OREGON TRIVIA

OREGON TRIVIA

COMPILED BY TED MAGNUSON

Rutledge Hill Press®
Nashville, Tennessee
A Thomas Nelson Company

Published by Rutledge Hill Press, a Thomas Nelson Company,
P. O. Box 141000, Nashville, Tennessee 37214.

Typography by Compass Communications, Inc., Nashville, Tennessee.

Library of Congress Cataloging-in-Publication Data

Magnuson, Ted, 1951–
    Oregon trivia / compiled by Ted Magnuson.
       p.   cm.
    ISBN 1-55853-601-9
    1. Oregon—Miscellanea.   2. Questions and answers.
I. Title.
F876.5.M34   1998
979.5'043'076—dc21   99-15449
                                     CIP

Printed in the United States of America
2 3 4 5 6 7 8 9—05 04 03 02 01 00

TABLE OF CONTENTS

PREFACE 7

GEOGRAPHY 11

ENTERTAINMENT 41

HISTORY 71

ARTS & LITERATURE 103

SPORTS & LEISURE 131

SCIENCE & NATURE 161

PREFACE

Oregon is a land of contrasts. It is a place where tall timber and snow-capped mountains shadow high deserts, and spawning salmon and foraging bears coexist with major universities and burgeoning cities. It is a place where the sounds of world-class theater and music blend with the songs of whales as they migrate along a spectacular coastline dotted with towering capes and wide, sandy beaches. Once the destination at the end of the trail for rugged pioneers, Oregon boasts a culturally rich and diverse population. It is a place where small wineries stand adjacent to high-tech corporations, where Native American place-names are pronounced with care, and where such important initiatives as health care and environmental conservation first took root.

Oregon Trivia is designed to be informative, educational, and entertaining. But most of all, I hope you will be motivated to learn more about the great state of Oregon. Enjoy.

—Ted Magnuson

OREGON
TRIVIA

GEOGRAPHY

Q. What marks the southern border of Oregon?

A. Forty-second parallel of latitude.

Q. In what direction does the Willamette River flow?

A. North, as do the Deschutes and the John Day.

Q. What hazard to shipping is located at the mouth of the Columbia River?

A. One of the most dangerous bars in the world.

Q. What is the highest and largest exposed fault in North America and second-largest in the world at 30 miles?

A. Abert Rim.

Q. Chain-saw sculptures people what entire town?

A. Sea Gulch, created by sawyer Ray Kowalski, near Seal Rock.

Q. The Oregon Trail crosses what mountain range between Ontario and La Grande?

A. Blue Mountains.

—————

Q. In what time zone is Oregon?

A. Pacific, except Ontario, which is in the Mountain Time Zone.

—————

Q. How many major hydropower dams are in Oregon?

A. Three: Bonneville, the Dalles, and John Day.

—————

Q. What reservoir was formed at the confluence of the Metolius, Deschutes, and Crooked Rivers?

A. Lake Billy Chinook.

—————

Q. Who was the Oregon City of Burns named after?

A. Scottish poet Robert Burns.

—————

Q. What is a haystack rock?

A. A cape eroded by wave action and seismic activity that resembles a haystack standing in the surf.

—————

Q. What natural feature near the Crooked River is popular with rock climbers?

A. Smith Rocks.

Q. How did the town of Hebo get its name?

A. From Mount Hebo, said to have been *"heaved* up high, *ho!"*

Q. The McNary and Owyhee Dams have what primary function?

A. Irrigation.

Q. North of Ontario, what marks the eastern border of Oregon?

A. Snake River.

Q. What is the origin of the name of the town Indanha?

A. An early hotel on the site that was named after Idan-Ha, a popular Idaho resort and mineral springs.

Q. What is the largest city in Oregon?

A. Portland, followed by Eugene and Salem.

Q. What basalt extrusion rises above surrounding sedimentary rocks in Clatsop County?

A. Onion Peak.

Q. How many lighthouses are on the Oregon coast?

A. Nine: Tillamook Rock, Cape Meares, Yaquina Head, Yaquina Bay, Heceta Head, Umpqua River, Cape Arago, Coquille River, and Cape Blanco.

Q. Where is the largest lava flow in the United States?

A. Jordan Crater in Malheur County.

———⊛———

Q. How big are the Oregon Caves?

A. Passageways extend 3.5 miles; the largest room measures 240 feet long, 50 feet wide, and 40 feet high.

———⊛———

Q. How many covered bridges are in Oregon?

A. Forty-nine.

———⊛———

Q. In addition to a river, the eastern border of the state is marked by what meridian?

A. 117 west.

———⊛———

Q. What highway extends along the entire length of Oregon's coast?

A. U.S. 101.

———⊛———

Q. What type of rock is found in the Oregon Caves?

A. Marble.

———⊛———

Q. According to the 1990 census, how many Native Americans live in Oregon?

A. 34,496, a little over 1 percent of the population.

Q. How does Oregon rank among the states in size?

A. Tenth largest.

———❦———

Q. How high is Multnomah Falls?

A. 620 feet.

———❦———

Q. In 1845 which two Oregon pioneers named Portland by flipping a coin?

A. Asa Lovejoy and Francis Pettygrove, who wanted to name the site after their respective hometowns of Boston, Massachusetts, and Portland, Maine.

———❦———

Q. The Willamette Valley encompasses how large an area?

A. More than 2,500 square miles (100 miles long and 20 to 30 miles wide).

———❦———

Q. Who named Cape Disappointment and Deception Bay?

A. Capt. John Meares, who sought "the Great River of the West" but didn't recognize it when he anchored outside the bar at the mouth of the Columbia River.

———❦———

Q. Where might one find an old-growth cedar swamp?

A. Rockaway, believed to be the last existing expanse of such a wetland.

———❦———

Q. What are the Klamath Falls?

A. A rapid on the Link River that can be seen only when the reservoir is lowered during extended rainy weather.

Q. Why is the island in the lower Columbia River now called Sauvie Island rather than Sauvie's Island?

A. The government has eliminated apostrophes and possessives in mapmaking.

———⟨⟩———

Q. Who was Laurent Sauvie?

A. A retired Hudson's Bay Company trapper who operated a small dairy on Sauvie Island some 150 years ago.

———⟨⟩———

Q. In the early years, what was Corvallis called?

A. Marysville.

———⟨⟩———

Q. How many Camp Creeks are in Oregon?

A. Five: in Clackamas, Douglas, Lane (two), and Wallowa Counties.

———⟨⟩———

Q. What popular summer camp is situated on Mount Hood near Bull Run?

A. Camp Numanu.

———⟨⟩———

Q. Who wrote in his ship's log, "When we were over the bar, we found this to be a large river of fresh water, up which we steered"?

A. Capt. Robert Gray of *The Columbia*.

———⟨⟩———

Q. Standing 93 feet high, what is Oregon's tallest lighthouse?

A. Yaquina Head Lighthouse in the Yaquina Head Outstanding Natural Area.

Q. What is the name of the largest room in the Oregon Caves?

A. Ghost Room.

———∞∞———

Q. Why is Portland's water reservoir called Bull Run?

A. In pioneer days, wild (escaped) cattle roamed the area.

———∞∞———

Q. How large is Oregon?

A. 97,061 square miles.

———∞∞———

Q. How long is the Willamette River?

A. 309 miles.

———∞∞———

Q. Oregon comprises how many counties?

A. Thirty-six.

———∞∞———

Q. What were the original borders of the Oregon Territory, as organized by Congress in 1848?

A. All land west of the Continental Divide between 42 and 49 degrees north latitude.

———∞∞———

Q. What was the population of Oregon in 1996?

A. More than 3,181,000.

Q. Where is the largest urban wilderness in the nation?

A. Portland (Forest Park in the Tualatin Mountains contains 4,900 acres).

———∞∞∞———

Q. For whom was the eastern Oregon town of Joseph named?

A. Chief Joseph of the Nez Percé tribe.

———∞∞∞———

Q. What Wallowa County lake is an important watering hole for waterfowl?

A. Downey.

———∞∞∞———

Q. What region was an earlier settler describing when he wrote, "Rain rarely falls, even in the winter season, but the dews are sufficiently heavy to compensate for its absence"?

A. Willamette Valley.

———∞∞∞———

Q. What is the derivation of Camp Numanu's name?

A. A Native American word (possibly Chinook) meaning "beaver."

———∞∞∞———

Q. What happened to the population of Portland in the five years after the Lewis and Clark Centennial Explosion?

A. It doubled.

———∞∞∞———

Q. Crater Lake formed in the caldera of what volcano that erupted in prehistoric times?

A. Mount Mazama, which was estimated to be over 12,000 feet high.

Q. How did the Oregon Dunes form?

A. By volcanic action that lifted the region from the sea floor.

Q. When did Crater Lake become a national park?

A. In 1902.

Q. Who was instrumental in preserving Crater Lake as a national treasure?

A. William Gladstone Steel, who as a Kansas schoolboy read about the natural wonder in a newspaper used to wrap his lunch and later lobbied 17 years to pass the legislation.

Q. Which lighthouses on the Oregon coast no longer have a functioning light?

A. Tillamook Rock (now a privately owned columbarium) and Coquille River (solar-powered ornamental light only).

Q. In addition to the earthquakes of 1993, how many other significant quakes have shaken Oregon since World War II?

A. Three: Portland (1962) and the Puget Sound area (1949 and 1965).

Q. Where is colorful mountain man Joe Meek buried?

A. Old Scotch Church, north of Hillsboro.

Q. According to the 1997–98 *Oregon Blue Book*, how many of the state's communities experienced more than 30 percent population growth in the 1990s?

A. About 36.

Q. Where was the hottest temperature in Oregon recorded?

A. Pendleton (119 degrees, August 10, 1898).

Q. How did Chanticleer Point receive its name?

A. From an inn that stood on the site from 1912 to 1931.

Q. How many Johnson Creeks are in Oregon?

A. Six: southeast and southwest Portland; and Grant, Morrow, Umatilla, and Wallowa Counties.

Q. For whom was the town of Vernonia named?

A. Verona, daughter of co-founder Ozias Cherrington.

Q. Oregon's Benton County was named in honor of what American?

A. Thomas Hart Benton, U.S. senator from Missouri and long-time Oregon Territory advocate.

Q. What organization gave Wahkeena Falls its present name?

A. Mazamas Trail Club, in 1915.

Q. For whom was the town of Shaniko named?

A. August Sherneckau, an early settler.

Q. What town, reputedly the wildest in frontier times, experienced a range war between sheep ranchers and cattle ranchers?

A. Prineville.

Q. In 1844 what was the town that became Portland called?

A. Stumptown, after the tree stumps littering the site.

Q. Of communities over 10,000 population, what Oregon town experienced the largest rate of growth during the 1990s?

A. Troutdale, at 62 percent (from 7,852 residents to 12,750).

Q. Why was Crater Lake unknown to early explorers and settlers?

A. Tribal shamans forbade most Native Americans to view the lake, so they said nothing about it.

Q. According to travel writers and author Lewis Freeman, what are the only two rivers with "the audacity to gouge a course straight through a range of mountains"?

A. The Columbia, which plows through the Cascades, and the Brahmaputra, which cuts a swath through the Himalayas from Tibet to the Bay of Bengal.

Q. What primary obstacle did the Columbia Gorge present to early settlers?

A. The Cascades, a series of rapids that made the downstream journey risky.

Q. What was the first device used to measure the depth of Crater Lake by sounding?

A. Piano wire, in 1886 (U.S. Geological Survey sounded 1,996 feet).

———— ∞∞∞ ————

Q. What kind of fish are in Crater Lake?

A. Rainbow trout and kokanee salmon, stocked from 1888 to 1941 because the lake contained no native fish.

———— ∞∞∞ ————

Q. The spot where the Willamette and Columbia Rivers meet has what name?

A. Kelley Point.

———— ∞∞∞ ————

Q. What famous newspaperman first climbed Mount Hood on July 11, 1857?

A. Henry Pittock, along with Lyman Chittendom, Wilbur Cornell, and Rev. T. A. Wood.

———— ∞∞∞ ————

Q. Who named the Deschutes River?

A. French Canadian trappers of the Hudson's Bay Company.

———— ∞∞∞ ————

Q. Where can evidence be seen of dinosaurs, saber-toothed tigers, crocodiles, rhinos, camels, and horses with toes?

A. John Day Fossil Beds National Monument.

———— ∞∞∞ ————

Q. How is the climate of western Oregon officially described?

A. West Coast marine.

Q. How did the town of Yachats (YAH-hots) receive its name?

A. From the Yachats tribe (the name means "foot of hill").

Q. Why is the bridge over the Columbia River at Cascade Locks called the "Bridge of the Gods"?

A. It is named for a legendary Native American land bridge.

Q. What is the name of the island in Crater Lake?

A. Wizard Island.

Q. What is the capital of Oregon?

A. Salem.

Q. Why are the Cascades of the Columbia no longer visible?

A. They were flooded when Bonneville Dam was built.

Q. What was the first capital of the Oregon Territory?

A. Oregon City, 1848-1850.

Q. How did the town of Scappoose come by its name?

A. From the Chinook word for "gravely plain."

Q. How did the first steamboats negotiate the Columbia River's Cascades rapids?

A. They didn't; prior to construction of the Cascade Locks, passengers and freight portaged around the Cascades via a railroad.

Q. What Oregon place-name means "many fish"?

A. Neskowin.

Q. Where in Oregon can one ski year-round?

A. Palmer Glacier, Mount Hood.

Q. Which Oregon river has headwaters in the Anthony Lakes?

A. Grande Ronde.

Q. What is the deepest lake in the United States?

A. Crater Lake, at 1,932 feet.

Q. What was an early name of Forest Grove?

A. West Tualatin Plains.

Q. From what did the city of Tillamook derive its name?

A. Tillamook band of Salish Indians.

Q. How was the correct depth of Crater Lake finally determined?

A. Sonar.

———⊗⊗⊗———

Q. For whom was the town of Mikkalo named?

A. John Mikkalo, an early settler.

———⊗⊗⊗———

Q. How many John Day Rivers are in Oregon?

A. Two: the larger is in eastern Oregon and the other is in Clatsop County.

———⊗⊗⊗———

Q. What is America's deepest gorge?

A. Hells Canyon, averaging 6,600 feet deep for 40 miles and measuring 7,993 feet from He Devil Mountain to Granite Creek below.

———⊗⊗⊗———

Q. According to the 1997–98 *Oregon Blue Book,* what is the state's fastest-growing village?

A. Granite, 50 miles southeast of Pendleton (three-fold increase, from 8 people to 25 people).

———⊗⊗⊗———

Q. What was the second capital of the Oregon Territory?

A. Salem, beginning in 1850.

———⊗⊗⊗———

Q. How does the Columbia compare with other American rivers in length?

A. Third-longest, flowing 1,242 miles with a total drop of 2,654 feet.

Q. By what other name was the town of Neskowin once known?

A. Marx (1904-1910).

———

Q. What town is named after a nearby bald peak that Native Americans called "home of eagles"?

A. Yoncalla.

———

Q. How many mountain ranges are in Oregon?

A. Eleven.

———

Q. Where can one find America's tallest Douglas fir tree?

A. Coast Range near Coos Bay (Finnegan's Fir, 302 feet tall).

———

Q. How many years of geological history are viewable at the John Day Fossil Beds?

A. 45 million to 50 million.

———

Q. What Oregon place-name means "three-legged fishnet holder"?

A. Wallowa.

———

Q. What is the highest point in Oregon?

A. Mount Hood, at 11,235 feet.

Q. What was an early name for Irrigon?

A. Stokes.

Q. What is the state's largest county in area?

A. Harney, in southeastern Oregon.

Q. What helped make the geological record clear at the John Day Fossil Beds?

A. Volcanic ash, which buried the plants and animals, preserving them immediately.

Q. What Oregon place-name means "little apples" in Spanish?

A. Manzanita.

Q. What is volcanic ash?

A. Rock pulverized by volcanic action that falls to earth like snow.

Q. For whom was the city of Condon named?

A. Harvey C. Condon, an Arlington attorney, town-site developer, and nephew of Thomas Condon.

Q. How does Multnomah Falls rank in height among America's waterfalls?

A. Tied for fifth (behind Yosemite, Ribbon, Silver Strand, Feather, and equal to Bridalveil, all in California).

Q. What is the state's smallest county in area?

A. Multnomah, in northwestern Oregon.

Q. For whom was Marquam Hill named?

A. Philip A. Marquam, lawyer and Multnomah County judge.

Q. Who discovered the John Day Fossil Beds?

A. Rev. Thomas Condon.

Q. What Oregon municipality is known as the "Rose City"?

A. Portland.

Q. Who pioneered the road over Mount Hood that enabled settlers to bring their wagons into the Willamette Valley?

A. Samuel K. Barlow (Barlow Road).

Q. What is the name of the governor's mansion in Salem?

A. Mahonia.

Q. Jennings Lodge was named for whom?

A. Berryman Jennings, a receiver in the Oregon City land office and one of three partners in the *Lot Whitcomb,* the first steamboat launched on the Willamette River.

Q. What are the 11 largest mountain ranges in the state?

A. Cascade, Coast, Steens, Wallowas, Blue, Strawberry, Siskiyous, Pueblo Mountains, Mahogany, Trout Creek, and Wagontire Mountain.

Q. According to geographer Louis McArthur, for whom were the Paulina Mountains, Paulina Creek, and Paulina Lake named?

A. A belligerent Snake chief who was killed in 1867.

Q. U.S. 99 between Sherwood and Newberg is known by what name?

A. Herbert Hoover Memorial Highway.

Q. What interstate highways cross Oregon?

A. I-84 (east/west) and I-5 (north/south).

Q. What is Oregon's tallest building?

A. Wells Fargo Building in Portland, at 546 feet (formerly First Interstate Bank Tower).

Q. What is unique about Gilchrist in Klamath County?

A. It is one of the lumber industry's last "company towns."

Q. How many students attended public school in Oregon in 1996?

A. Approximately 561,500.

Q. What is the largest clear-span wood structure in the world?

A. The blimp hangar at the former Tillamook Naval Air Station.

Q. How much of Oregon is classified as desert?

A. Twenty-five percent, including the Alvord and High Deserts.

Q. Where can one find the longest covered bridge in Oregon?

A. Northwest of Oakridge; the 180-foot Office Bridge spans the North Fork of the Willamette and originally connected a lumber mill with its office.

Q. Of what was Judge Matthew Deady speaking when he said, "Its construction contributed more . . . to Oregon than any other achievement prior to the building of the railroads in 1870"?

A. Barlow Road.

Q. What is the state's largest lake?

A. Upper Klamath, covering 58,922 acres.

Q. From what famed Alpine landmark does the tallest peak in the Wallowa Mountains derive its name?

A. Matterhorn.

Q. The name of what town was inspired by its location in the middle of a long and straight stretch of railroad track?

A. Tangent.

Q. How was Sam Barlow repaid for his efforts at road-building?

A. Toll charges.

Q. The name of what city means "down the river" in the Chinook language?

A. Multnomah.

Q. According to some geographers, how many mountains constitute a mountain range in Oregon?

A. One; solitary Wagontire Mountain (6,504 feet), straddling Lake and Harney Counties, is generally considered a "range."

Q. What is the fifth-deepest lake in the world?

A. Crater Lake.

Q. What is Oregon's major agricultural crop?

A. Nursery stock.

Q. What U.S. highway crosses the Nehalem River?

A. U.S. 26, the "Sunset Highway."

Q. After Alaska and Hawaii were admitted to the Union, what did Oregon become?

A. Geographical center of the United States.

Q. Who named Cape Foulweather?

A. Capt. James Cook, in March 1778.

Q. What served as a landmark for early Oregon surveyors?

A. Willamette Stone, near Burnside.

Q. What are the river tributaries of the Deschutes?

A. White, Metolius, and Crooked.

Q. How many airports, heliports, and landing surfaces are in Oregon?

A. About 400, including 34 general aviation airports.

Q. Why is the Willamette Meridian so named?

A. It marks the longitude of the Willamette River as it flows through Portland.

Q. How many mountain ranges are in Harney County?

A. Four: Steens, Trout Creek, Pueblo, and Wagontire Mountain.

Q. Where is Jacksonville located?

A. In the foothills of the Siskiyou Mountains.

Q. What is the Native American meaning of the place-name Nehalem?

A. "Place of peace": *ne*, the prefix for "place," and *halem*, the word for "peace."

———∞———

Q. What is the derivation of Eagle Point's name?

A. It was suggested by John Matthews in 1872 because of a crag north of town where eagles roosted.

———∞———

Q. What town hosts the annual Concours d'Elegance antique auto show on the grounds of its university?

A. Forest Grove.

———∞———

Q. For whom were Harney Lake, Harney Valley, and Harney County named?

A. Brig. Gen. William Selby Harney, a popular soldier, Indian fighter, and Civil War commander.

———∞———

Q. How many Haystack Rocks are in Oregon?

A. Three: off Cannon Beach, off Cape Kiwanda, and in Wallowa County.

———∞———

Q. What site gives botanists their money's worth of vegetation?

A. Eight Dollar Mountain near Grants Pass, known for its rich diversity of plant life.

———∞———

Q. What two men were Berryman Jennings's partners in the construction and launching of the steamboat *Lot Whitcomb*?

A. Lot Whitcomb and S. S. White.

Q. The town of Amity received its name as the result of what event?

A. Two nearby towns pooled their resources to build a school-house there in 1849.

Q. Whose name is remembered in Roseburg?

A. Aaron Rose, the popular tavernkeeper for whom the town was named shortly after his death.

Q. What park is especially designed for the blind?

A. Oral Hull Park, near Sandy.

Q. What towns vied to be the seat of Douglas County?

A. Roseburg and Winchester.

Q. What is the significance of the Sunset Highway's name?

A. It is was named in honor of the U.S. Army's 41st Infantry (Sunset) Division for its service during World War II.

Q. Why was Junction City so named?

A. In 1870 it was the site where Ben Holladay planned to connect his railroads.

Q. By what other names was the Washington County seat of Hillsboro known?

A. East Tualatin Plain, Hillsborough, Columbia, and Columbus.

Q. What town was known as West Tualatin Plain?

A. Forest Grove.

———⊗⊗⊗———

Q. What group is recognized at Crown Point in the Columbia Gorge?

A. Pioneers who settled Oregon.

———⊗⊗⊗———

Q. In what recent years have floods affected the lower Willamette Valley?

A. 1964, 1974, and 1996.

———⊗⊗⊗———

Q. How often does the name Hole in the Ground appear among Oregon place-names?

A. Twice: in Douglas County and Lake County.

———⊗⊗⊗———

Q. How did The Dalles come by its name?

A. French voyageurs called the area where the Columbia River narrowed and spilled over rapids *les dalles,* or "the trough."

———⊗⊗⊗———

Q. What are the three largest towns of Oregon's bay area?

A. Coos Bay, North Bend, and Charleston.

———⊗⊗⊗———

Q. From what port is more lumber shipped than from any other in the world?

A. Coos Bay.

Q. Who was the founder of Milwaukee, Oregon?

A. Lot Whitcomb.

Q. By what name was Roseburg known prior to 1857?

A. Deer Creek.

Q. How high did the Willamette River crest in the flood of 1996?

A. 28.5 feet above normal (10 feet over flood stage) at Portland; 35.1 feet (7 feet over flood stage) at Salem.

Q. What hardwood, used for plaques, bowls, and other decorative pieces, grows only on Oregon's southern coast?

A. Myrtlewood.

Q. How did Timothy Lake receive its name?

A. The reservoir flooded Timothy Meadow, so-named by sheepherders who sowed timothy grass there to feed their sheep.

Q. What is the largest lake on the Oregon coast?

A. Siltcoos.

Q. Where are prime locations for rock-hounding?

A. Beaches, river bars between Salem and Corvallis, and road cuts near Ashland, Madras, and Prineville.

Q. What is Oregon's "tallest town"?

A. Lakeview (elevation 4,800 feet).

Q. What town is the starting point for river trips on the Grande Ronde?

A. Elgin.

Q. How high above mean sea level is the top of the Tillamook Rock lighthouse, three miles out to sea from Ecola Park?

A. 130 feet.

Q. What is the main thoroughfare for the Baker County mining district?

A. Elk Horn Drive.

Q. The Willamette River has how many primary tributaries?

A. Fourteen. (Tualatin, Yamhill, Luckiamute, Marys River, Long Tom, Suislaw, Clackamas, Mollala, Pudding, Calapooia, Santiam, McKenzie, Coast Fork, and Middle Fork.)

Q. What river flows through Pendleton?

A. Umatilla.

Q. If the north border of Oregon followed the Columbia River and did not stop at the 47th parallel, what Washington city would be in Oregon?

A. Walla Walla.

Q. Why is Farewell Bend so named?

A. Pioneers left the Snake River there to follow the southern uplands of the Powder River Valley.

Q. What Oregon city has a Lakeshore Drive, Michigan Avenue, Division Street, and Washburn Way?

A. Klamath Falls.

Q. How did Lookingglass Creek on the Grande Ronde in Umatilla and Union Counties get its name?

A. It is named for a Nez Percé chief who was known for carrying a small pocket mirror.

Q. Where does the Coast Range join the Cascades?

A. Spurs of the cascade Range join the Coast Range south of the Suislaw River, and the ranges become fully merged in the Klamath Mountains.

Q. Who championed the cause of building a highway along the Oregon coast?

A. Ben F. Jones, for whom a bridge over Rocky Creek north of Newport is named.

Q. How many Black Buttes can be found in Oregon?

A. Two: the most prominent Black Butte, symmetrical and dark in color, is a landmark on the Jefferson-Deschutes county line in the Cascade Range; Lane County also boosts a Black Butte.

Q. What did the Nez Percé Indians call the Grand Ronde Valley?

A. *Cop Copi,* or "Valley of Peace."

Q. How many natural features in the state are named Bingham?

A. Four: Bingham Creek in Douglas County, Bingham Lake in Klamath County, Bingham Mountain in Coos County, and Bingham Springs in Umatilla County.

Q. The name of what Oregon town was derived from the title of an unfinished book by Robert Louis Stevenson?

A. Hermiston (from *The Weir of Hermiston*).

Q. Where can one find the Yampo School?

A. In the Eola Hills on the YAMhill-POlk County line.

Q. By what other names was Frenchglen called?

A. Somerange (for summer cattle grazing on the range).

Q. How many Bunker Hills can be found in Oregon?

A. Three: in Linn, Marion, and Coos Counties.

Q. What natural attraction on the North Umpqua River in Douglas County takes its name from the Chinook word for "graceful"?

A. Toketee Falls.

ENTERTAINMENT

Q. In 1992 how much did the film and video industry contribute to Oregon's economy?

A. $61 million.

———∞∞———

Q. How many carousel animals are owned by the International Museum of Carousel Art in Portland?

A. 700.

———∞∞———

Q. What 1979 film about a rodeo cowboy included scenes of Ontario?

A. *Bronco Billy,* starring Clint Eastwood and Sandra Locke.

———∞∞———

Q. What is a Pig N' Ford race?

A. An event in which contestants sprint to a pigpen, grab a pig, put it in the back of a Model T pickup, drive a lap around the track, and grab another pig, repeated three times.

———∞∞———

Q. What is the birthplace of trumpeter Doc Severinsen, long-time music director of NBC-TV's *Tonight Show?*

A. Arlington.

Q. Where did Debbie Reynolds go "over the falls" in the movie *How the West Was Won*?

A. Graves Creek section of the Rogue River.

—⊱⊰—

Q. What town serves as a starting point for many jet-boat tours of Hell's Canyon?

A. Oxbow.

—⊱⊰—

Q. Where is the Alpenfest held?

A. The communities of Wallowa Lake in late summer.

—⊱⊰—

Q. What 1993 movie featured Meryl Streep as a Rogue River runner?

A. *The River Wild.*

—⊱⊰—

Q. Where was noted food writer James Beard born?

A. Portland.

—⊱⊰—

Q. Oregon scenes were featured in what movie about a gang of surfers who robbed banks while wearing masks with faces of ex-presidents?

A. *Point Break.*

—⊱⊰—

Q. What state park was originally a military outpost built to defend Oregon from a Confederate naval attack?

A. Fort Stevens.

Q. What movie filmed in Oregon features an author on book tour? Phil Knight, Garrison Keillor, and Studs Terkel play themselves in the film.

A. *The Big One.*

———— ∞∞∞ ————

Q. Of all Oregon wines, which variety has received most international acclaim?

A. Pinot Noir.

———— ∞∞∞ ————

Q. In what film did a retired pro football player discover he can still make a difference with troubled teens as a high school coach?

A. *Reggie's Prayer,* filmed in Portland in 1996.

———— ∞∞∞ ————

Q. For several weeks each June, what Portland celebration features spectacular parades, a carnival midway, a pageant, visiting navy ships, air shows, and an auto race?

A. Rose Festival, which also includes a renowned traditional rose show.

———— ∞∞∞ ————

Q. Where may one see a 33-foot model showing how the Columbia River flowed prior to the construction of hydro-electric dams?

A. Discovery Center in the Dalles.

———— ∞∞∞ ————

Q. Portland-based animator Will Vinton, James Whitmore, and Halley's Comet all contributed to what amusing 1984 film?

A. *The Adventures of Mark Twain.*

Q. What town hosts an annual Crawfish Festival?

A. Tualatin.

———∞———

Q. The book *Tying and Fishing the Fuzzy Nymphs* by what Chiloquin fly-fisherman has been printed four times?

A. Polly Rosborough.

———∞———

Q. Kevin Costner starred in what 1997 movie set in 2013 A.D. and filmed in central Oregon?

A. *The Postman.*

———∞———

Q. When did the City of Portland become the owner of Civic Stadium?

A. 1965.

———∞———

Q. Susan St. James, Jessica Lange, and Jane Curtin took the bite out of inflation in what 1978 film?

A. *How to Beat the High Cost of Living,* filmed in Eugene.

———∞———

Q. What were used for bar stools at the old Battle Axe Inn on Mount Hood?

A. Tree stumps.

———∞———

Q. How did the Empire Block, built in 1907 and home of the Pendleton Underground Tours, get its name?

A. Owners Henry Schwartz and Frank Greulich named it after their business, the Empire Meat Market.

Q. Madonna was convicted of murder in what 1992 movie filmed in Oregon's largest city?

A. *Body of Evidence.*

Q. What 13-part Japanese television series was filmed in Oregon in 1984?

A. *Oregon Kara Ai (From Oregon, With Love).*

Q. How much revenue has Oregon realized from films, videos, and commercials each year since 1992?

A. An average of $33 million.

Q. Where did the Oregon filming take place for the 1978 movie titled *1941*?

A. Cannon Beach.

Q. Where are the annual Pig N' Ford races held?

A. Tillamook County Fair.

Q. Ryan O'Neal played in what 1997 thriller filmed in Portland?

A. *Zero Effect.*

Q. What is the signature of the Columbia Gorge Hotel's farm breakfast?

A. "Honey from the sky," poured over biscuits from shoulder height.

Q. What 1973 movie supposedly set in the Himalayas and based on a novel by James Hilton was filmed on Mt. Hood and in other locales in the western United States?

A. *Lost Horizon,* starring Charles Boyer, John Gielgud, and Liv Ullman.

Q. What town is known for its Octoberfest?

A. Mount Angel.

Q. The submarine USS *Blueback,* now on display at the Oregon Museum of Science and Industry in Portland, appeared in what hit movie?

A. *The Hunt for Red October.*

Q. What farm in Portland's West Hills features a velodrome, junior formula racetrack, and Little League diamonds with bleachers?

A. Alpenrose Dairy.

Q. In what 1991 movie does a banker realize just how diverse his company is when he reports to his new post: a small-town sperm bank.

A. *Frozen Assets,* filmed around Portland and the Columbia Gorge.

Q. What is Oregon's only drive-through park featuring exotic animals roaming free?

A. Wildlife Safari in Winston.

Q. How does Oregon differ from other states in its wine labeling requirements?

A. The variety of grape listed on the label must comprise 90 percent of the pulp used to make the wine (other states require only 75 percent).

Q. The exteriors of what resort appeared in the movie based on Stephen King's *The Shining*?

A. Timberline Lodge.

Q. Portland's KEX-AM 1190 first broadcast on what frequency when it went on the air in December 1926?

A. 670 AM.

Q. On what three mountains are Oregon's most popular ski areas?

A. Mount Hood, Mount Bachelor, and Mount Ashland.

Q. Filmed on Oregon's north coast in 1981, what motion picture featured a ghost and a lighthouse?

A. *Hysterical.*

Q. Where may one find the Northwest's biggest collection of World War II fighter planes?

A. Tillamook Air Museum (at the former Naval Air Station south of Tillamook, off Highway 101).

Q. What movie starring Dee Wallace Stone and Cloris Leachman was filmed in Portland in 1986?

A. *Shadow Play.*

Q. In 1955 what did area citizens and service clubs use as a guide to reproduce Fort Clatsop, originally built by Lewis and Clark?

A. William Clark's sketch in his journal.

———— ∞ ————

Q. Filmed in Oregon in 1987, what movie featured Keanu Reeves and Michelle Meyrink?

A. *Permanent Record.*

———— ∞ ————

Q. Oregon has how many wineries?

A. About 120.

———— ∞ ————

Q. The Battle Axe Inn on Mount Hood was larger than today's Timberline Lodge when it was destroyed by fire in what year?

A. 1949.

———— ∞ ————

Q. What was the name of the McMenamin Brothers' first tavern, opened in 1974?

A. Produce Row Cafe, in the Southeast Industrial District of Portland.

———— ∞ ————

Q. Where may one see Native-American tule mat lodges, wicki-ups, a song chamber, and (during the summer) a living history of the tribes as portrayed in dance, crafts, and storytelling?

A. The Museum at Warm Springs, created by the Confederated Tribes of Warm Springs.

Q. Based on the work of a Spanish author and filmed in Cannon Beach by a German production company, what 1995 motion picture won two awards at the Thessalonica film festival?

A. *Things I Never Told You.*

Q. How many Portland High Schools send representatives to the Rose Festival Court?

A. Fourteen.

Q. In 1979 what novelist pitched Pendleton to Hollywood producers as a great place to shoot a movie?

A. Ken Kesey.

Q. What towns annually host major gem and mineral shows?

A. Sweet Home, Eugene, Medford, and Roseburg.

Q. What was Oregon's first movie, directed by and featuring Buster Keaton?

A. *The General.*

Q. What was the first microbrewery to open in Portland since Prohibition?

A. Hillsdale Brewery and Public House, in 1984.

Q. Who created the Barbie doll?

A. Oregonian Bill Barton.

Q. What 1955 western filmed on the Oregon desert starred Walter Matthau and Kirk Douglas?

A. *The Indian Fighter.*

———∞∞∞———

Q. What movie filmed in Portland and directed by Oregonian Gus Van Sant stars Robin Williams?

A. *Don't Worry, He Won't Get Far on Foot.*

———∞∞∞———

Q. What 1965 big-screen comedy filmed along the Oregon coast featured Tony Curtis as the hero and Peter Falk and Jack Lemmon as the villains?

A. *The Great Race.*

———∞∞∞———

Q. Who directed *Good Will Hunting*?

A. Oregonian Gus Van Sant.

———∞∞∞———

Q. Who reigns over the Rose Festival Court?

A. Queen of Rosaria.

———∞∞∞———

Q. In 1939 who played Lincoln in *Abe Lincoln in Illinois,* filmed in Eugene?

A. Raymond Massey.

———∞∞∞———

Q. What was the world's first UHF television station to initiate regular broadcasts?

A. Portland's KPTV-Channel 27, September 27, 1952.

Q. Where was the movie *Assassins* filmed in 1995?

A. Portland.

———&&&———

Q. What city has hosted the annual Miss Oregon pageant since 1946?

A. Seaside.

———&&&———

Q. Clint Eastwood had a signing role in what western musical filmed in northeast Oregon?

A. *Paint Your Wagon* (1970).

———&&&———

Q. What metro Portland woman starred in the 1970s TV series *The Bionic Woman*?

A. Lindsay Wagner.

———&&&———

Q. When going cross-country skiing, what should you leave in plain sight on the dashboard of your car?

A. A valid snow pass.

———&&&———

Q. In what 1970 film did Jack Nicholson portray a musician who worked on oil rigs?

A. *Five Easy Pieces.*

———&&&———

Q. Paul Newman directed what 1971 movie based on the saga of a logging family written by Oregon author Ken Kesey?

A. *Sometimes a Great Notion.*

Q. What is the oldest "motel" in Oregon?

A. Wolf Creek Tavern, 20 miles north of Grants Pass, originally a stagecoach stop.

———⊗———

Q. Filmed at Portland's Grant High in 1994, *Mr. Holland's Opus* starred what actor?

A. Richard Dreyfus.

———⊗———

Q. Where are the oldest vineyards in the state?

A. Honeywood in Salem and Henry Endres in Oregon City.

———⊗———

Q. What 1975 John Wayne movie filmed in Oregon's Blue Mountains featured Katharine Hepburn "reprising" her 1952 role in *The African Queen*?

A. *Rooster Cogburn.*

———⊗———

Q. From what location did the nation's first educational radio broadcast emanate on March 23, 1923, over KYG-AM?

A. Portland's Benson Polytechnic High School.

———⊗———

Q. Of the Oregon vineyards that still produce varietal wine grapes, which was the first to do so, in 1961?

A. Hillcrest, in Roseburg, planted by Richard Summer.

———⊗———

Q. Eugene provided the scenery for what 1978 film comedy featuring togas and food fights?

A. *Animal House.*

Q. How was Portland's UHF station KPTV able to begin broadcasting on VHF channel 12?

A. Through a merger with independent KLOR, which owned the frequency.

Q. Why do naval vessels visit the Portland Rose Festival each year?

A. The 1957 appearance of the submarine USS *Nautilus,* fresh from its historic polar voyage under Arctic ice, was so popular with patrons that the navy scheduled annual visits to the festival.

Q. When did the Mount Hood Festival of Jazz begin?

A. 1982, in Gresham.

Q. What 1952 western filmed on Mount Hood starred Jimmy Stewart, Julie Adams, Arthur Kennedy, and Rock Hudson?

A. *Bend in the River.*

Q. Before being returned to his native Icelandic waters, Keiko, the star of *Free Willy,* underwent rehabilitation at what facility?

A. Oregon Coast Aquarium in Newport.

Q. What is the nation's largest open-air crafts sales venue?

A. Portland's Saturday market.

Q. What 1980 movie featured Mariel Hemingway and Patrice Donelly as track athletes?

A. *Personal Best.*

Q. What is Oregon's largest vineyard?

A. Montinore Vineyard in Dilley.

———⊗⊗⊗———

Q. What U.S. president spent the night at Wolf Creek Tavern near Grants Pass?

A. Rutherford B. Hayes.

———⊗⊗⊗———

Q. Where may Civil War battle reenactments be seen each Labor Day?

A. Fort Stevens State Park near Warrenton.

———⊗⊗⊗———

Q. What was the subject of *Come See the Paradise,* filmed in Astoria, the Willamette Valley, and Portland?

A. Internment of Japanese Americans during World War II.

———⊗⊗⊗———

Q. What is the function of Portland's Royal Rosarians, founded in 1912 and whose members are known for their white suits and straw hats?

A. Promotion of the Rose Festival and other civic events.

———⊗⊗⊗———

Q. What 1975 movie starring Jack Nicholson won five Oscars?

A. *One Flew Over the Cuckoo's Nest,* filmed in Eugene and the Willamette Valley.

———⊗⊗⊗———

Q. What institution in Bend preserves, interprets, and recreates the legends, lore, and natural legacy of the high desert?

A. High Desert Museum, which includes the Chiles Center on the Spirit of the West and 20 acres of outdoor trails abounding with wildlife and other exhibits.

Q. What was the first race sanctioned by the American Automobile Club?

A. Portland Automobile Race, held on the last day of the Rose Festival in 1909.

Q. When did navy ships make their first appearance at the Portland Rose Festival?

A. 1928.

Q. Gus Van Sant directed what film about male prostitutes in Portland?

A. *My Own Private Idaho.*

Q. Who coined such tongue-in-cheek phrases as "People in Oregon don't tan in the summertime, they rust"?

A. James Cloutier, who screenprinted the quips on T-shirts around 1980.

Q. Construction of Timberline Lodge was overseen by what federal agency?

A. Works Progress Administration, a New Deal project established by President Franklin D. Roosevelt, who attended the resort's dedication on September 28, 1937.

Q. What coastal state park is especially set up for hikers and cyclists?

A. Oswald West, near Cape Falcon.

Q. Where was the 1909 Portland Automobile Race held?

A. East Multnomah County (banked turns can still be seen at Rose City Golf Course).

———⊙⊙⊙———

Q. Three family pets traipsed across Oregon in what 1993 remake of a 1963 movie?

A. *Homeward Bound.*

———⊙⊙⊙———

Q. Where did chef, gourmet, and author James Beard spend his early years?

A. Portland, where his family was involved in the hotel business.

———⊙⊙⊙———

Q. The voices of Walt Disney's animated characters Goofy and Pluto, as well as Grumpy in the movie *Snow White and the Seven Dwarfs,* were provided by what Jacksonville resident?

A. Vance Colvig.

———⊙⊙⊙———

Q. Where is the Antique Powerland Farm Fair held each August?

A. Brooks.

———⊙⊙⊙———

Q. The steepest gondola climb in America is located where?

A. Mount Howard.

———⊙⊙⊙———

Q. When did trolley cars return to Portland?

A. 1985, when the eastside MAX Light Rail Line was being built.

Q. What Walt Disney film featured footage of the 1974 Pendleton Round-Up?

A. *Twister, Bull from the Sky.*

———— ∞ ————

Q. Where was the nation's first ski area established?

A. Summit (opened December 11, 1927, operated by the Advertising Club of Portland).

———— ∞ ————

Q. What Newport eatery was featured in the film *Never Give an Inch,* starring Paul Newman and Henry Fonda?

A. Mo's.

———— ∞ ————

Q. In what year did the first ski jump open on Mount Hood?

A. 1928, when the Cascade Ski Club built the jump at Multorpor.

———— ∞ ————

Q. Multorpor is an acronym for what?

A. MULTnomah ORegon PORtland.

———— ∞ ————

Q. What problem resulted from seven Japanese destroyers that sailed to the 1968 Portland Rose Festival?

A. Ship berths were not immediately available because Mayor Terry Schrunk had not notified festival planners of his informal invitation to the flotilla.

———— ∞ ————

Q. When was the Pendleton Round-Up first held?

A. 1910, when local ranchers got together to see who had the best cowhands.

Q. Clark Gable and Loretta Young starred in what 1935 motion picture classic produced by Daryl F. Zanuck and filmed in Oregon?

A. *Call of the Wild.*

———∞———

Q. What is a popular winter outdoor activity along the Oregon coast?

A. Storm-watching.

———∞———

Q. What city hosts an annual Outdoor Quilt Show and High Mountain Dixieland Jazz Festival?

A. Sisters.

———∞———

Q. Where may one participate in the National Hang Gliding Contest?

A. Lakeview, on the Fourth of July.

———∞———

Q. What museum is dedicated to Arctic Circle art and artifacts?

A. Paul Jensen Arctic Museum in Monmouth.

———∞———

Q. In 1984 why did the citizens of Paisley organize an annual Mosquito Festival?

A. To raise money for mosquito control.

———∞———

Q. What movie, filmed in 1985 in Brownsville and Cottage Grove, was based on Stephen King's *The Body*?

A. *Stand By Me.*

Q. In what year did Oregon filmmaker Gus Van Sant release *Drugstore Cowboy?*

A. 1989.

Q. Portland's Metro Washington Park Zoo specializes in what major zoological program?

A. Breeding rare and endangered species, such as the Asian elephant and Humbolt penguin.

Q. When was Oregon's first commercial radio broadcast?

A. 1922, on station KGW from the Portland offices of *The Oregonian.*

Q. Who starred in *Great American Cowboy*, judged 1973's best documentary feature?

A. Larry Mahan of Brooks, six-time national rodeo champion.

Q. Where were *Free Willy, The Goonies,* and *Kindergarten Cop* filmed?

A. Astoria.

Q. What makes Lakeview a good location for hang gliding?

A. Excellent thermals produced by the town's close proximity to the southeast Oregon high desert.

Q. In 1941 what structure was erected in a record 23 days for the Pendleton Round-Up?

A. A concrete grandstand to replace the south grandstand, destroyed by fire just 27 days before the event.

Q. What is the notable achievement of Reed College graduate John G. Sperling, who received a doctorate in economic history from Cambridge University?

A. He reinvented the business school by founding the University of Phoenix in 1976.

———— ∞ ————

Q. What former central Oregon railhead is an accessible and fascinating ghost town?

A. Shaniko.

———— ∞ ————

Q. What festival is held late each summer in Grants Pass?

A. Jedediah Smith Mountain Man Rendezvous and Buffalo Barbecue.

———— ∞ ————

Q. What was the first building erected in Newport?

A. Ocean House, modeled on a hotel of the same name in Newport, Rhode Island.

———— ∞ ————

Q. What films were made in Wallowa County?

A. *Paint Your Wagon* and *Journey Home*.

———— ∞ ————

Q. What draws visitors to Scio the third week in May?

A. Northwest Champion Sheepdog Trials and the Lamb & Wool Festival.

———— ∞ ————

Q. Where is the Oregon Sports Hall of Fame?

A. Portland.

Q. Who is Matt Groenig?

A. Portland-born creator of the popular cartoon series *The Simpsons*.

———❧———

Q. What new form of animation did Will Vinton create?

A. Claymation, in which characters are formed from clay and manipulated between camera shots to simulate movement.

———❧———

Q. What are Peter Britt Festivals?

A. A series of events featuring a wide variety of music and dance that are held each June through September in Jacksonville.

———❧———

Q. Where were portions of the movie *Run* filmed in 1990?

A. Portland.

———❧———

Q. Oregon Dunes National Recreation Area covers how many acres?

A. About 32,000.

———❧———

Q. What is the Hoodoo Bowl?

A. A ski area on the Santiam Pass in the Cascades.

———❧———

Q. Bozo the Clown was created by what Medford resident?

A. Vance Colvig.

Q. Oregon Dunes National Recreation Area is part of what 630,000-acre spread?

A. Siuslaw National Forest.

Q. What coincides with the Hood River Valley Harvest Fest, celebrated in early October since 1983?

A. The beginning of the Mid-Columbia's fall foliage season.

Q. Where was Newport's 1866 Ocean House located?

A. On the site of the present-day Coast Guard Station.

Q. As an aviation promotion, who landed his plane at Swan Island on September 14, 1927?

A. Charles Lindbergh.

Q. What is the oldest frame house in the Pacific Northwest?

A. Jason Lee House in Salem, built in 1841.

Q. What TV series, filmed in Portland, chronicled the life of a female police detective?

A. *Under Suspicion.*

Q. What weekly newspaper began publication in 1891 and was continuously published by the same editor until 1944?

A. *Marshfield Sun.*

Q. Who wrote the book on which Gus Van Sant based the 1992 movie *Even Cowgirls Get the Blues*?

A. Tom Robbins.

Q. Heather Locklear starred in what movie filmed in Oregon's largest city in 1992?

A. *Body Language.*

Q. *The Oregonian* began publication in what year?

A. 1851.

Q. Where can one attend Carriage-Me-Back Days, a horse and buggy convocation?

A. Brownsville, the third weekend in April.

Q. Jennifer Irwin, the "Awesome Beach Girl" of *The Bikini Car Wash Company,* starred as Laura in what 1991 movie?

A. *Wild Child.*

Q. Where did "machine-rolled ice cream cones" make their debut?

A. 1904 Lewis and Clark Centennial Exposition.

Q. What 1992 movie shot in Portland and along the north coast featured a secretary from hell?

A. *The Temp.*

Q. What amusement park was billed as the "Coney Island of the West"?

A. Oaks Park in Portland, in operation since 1905.

Q. What 1977 movie featuring a shipwreck in the Aleutian Islands was actually filmed at Gold Beach?

A. *Sea Gypsies.*

Q. Where do trails named Cape Cove, The Trail of Restless Waters, and The Trail of the Whispering Spruce lead hikers to the Devil's Churn and Cook's Chasm?

A. On 800-foot-high Cape Perpetua, south of Yachats.

Q. Eugene and Corvallis were filming sites for what movie starring James and Josh Brolin that examined the issue of steroid abuse in high school?

A. *Finish Line.*

Q. Why do Jacksonville residents refer to the Jeremiah Nunan House, built in 1892, as the Catalogue House?

A. Because the dwelling was prefabricated in Knoxville, Tennessee, then shipped via 14 railroad boxcars and assembled as a Christmas present for Mrs. Nunan.

Q. Where can one go to see a turn-of-the-century newspaper and job printing shop?

A. *Marshfield Sun* Printing Museum in Coos Bay.

Q. In what movie filmed in Portland does Burt Reynolds teach Casey Siemaska everything he knows about safecracking?

A. *Breaking In.*

———— ✺ ————

Q. Founded in 1852, what gold-rush town has been designated a National Historic Landmark Community because of its collection of preserved pioneer buildings?

A. Jacksonville.

———— ✺ ————

Q. A mountain man's son was kidnapped in what 1988 film featuring scenes of the Grants Pass area?

A. *Spirit of the Eagle.*

———— ✺ ————

Q. Unemployment in the lumber industry was a catalyst for action in what movie filmed in Toledo in 1992?

A. *The Bed You Sleep In.*

———— ✺ ————

Q. What movie featuring Oregon scenes concerned a mad blimp driver who almost ruined the Super Bowl?

A. *Black Sunday.*

———— ✺ ————

Q. Who established the International Rose Test Gardens in 1917 in Washington Park and gave Portland its nickname, the "City of Roses"?

A. Jesse Curry.

———— ✺ ————

Q. In 1978 Mickey Rooney won an Oscar for best supporting actor in what movie containing scenes filmed along Oregon's north coast?

A. *The Black Stallion.*

Q. Space aliens chose loggers for diabolical biological studies in what movie filmed in Roseburg and Oakland in 1992?

A. *Fire in the Sky.*

———⊗———

Q. Where was the first Peter Britt Festival held?

A. Peter Britt Gardens at First and Pine Streets in Jacksonville.

———⊗———

Q. Jane Seymour played a black widow in what 1993 film made in Oregon?

A. *Praying Mantis.*

———⊗———

Q. How many waterfalls are in Silver Falls State Park?

A. Ten.

———⊗———

Q. Where did a film crew recreate the Scopes Monkey Trial for a 1987 television version of *Inherit the Wind*?

A. Jacksonville.

———⊗———

Q. What TV series featuring a ranch family was filmed near Bend in 1994?

A. *McKenna.*

———⊗———

Q. What event held each August in Eugene features performances of an eclectic blend of American music composed by the likes of Amy Beach, Charles Ives, Duke Ellington, and Cole Porter?

A. Oregon Festival of American Music.

Q. What festival held each September at Drake Park in Bend showcases symphonic, Broadway, and big-band music?

A. Cascade Music Festival.

———∞———

Q. Dory Days, a festival featuring dory demonstrations, a simulated dory rescue, food, crafts, and a barn dance, has been held each July since 1960 in what city?

A. Pacific City.

———∞———

Q. What is the name of Eugene's performing arts venue?

A. Hult Center for the Performing Arts, built in 1982.

———∞———

Q. What is the seating capacity of Silva Concert Hall at the Hult Center in Eugene?

A. 2,500.

———∞———

Q. As of 1998, Mildred Davy, 87-year-old general manager of KTIL-AM 1590 in Tillamook, has hosted the station's *It's a Woman's World* program for how many years?

A. Thirty-six.

———∞———

Q. What is the name of Jim Alde's whale sculpture in Yachats that features a metal tail and a back formed by a mound of earth, and spouts water every 60 seconds during daylight hours?

A. *Bazalgette.*

Q. What is the seating capacity of the Intermediate Theatre in the Portland Center for the Performing Arts?

A. 960.

───────※───────

Q. What fraternal insurance company's acronym is included in the name of WOW Hall, located at Eighth and Lincoln in Eugene?

A. Woodmen of the World.

───────※───────

Q. What event attracts thousands of bird-watchers to the Malheur Wildlife Refuge each April?

A. John Schert Migratory Bird Festival and Art Show.

───────※───────

Q. Where can one find Terwilliger Hot Springs, the Delta Old Growth Nature Trail, the Willamette River Gorge, and the Westfir covered bridge?

A. On the Aufderheide Memorial Drive (Box Canyon Road) in the McKenzie River Valley.

───────※───────

Q. What site might gardeners and flower fans enjoy in Lincoln City?

A. Connie Hansen Garden, which features beautiful rhododendrons, azaleas, irises, primroses, and several varieties of trees and perennials.

───────※───────

Q. Where can one enjoy the thrills of sailplaning and "sand sailing"?

A. Alvord Desert.

Q. For what local specialties are the Otis Cafe and the Java Depot in Lincoln City best known?

A. Otis Cafe bakes a tasty molasses bread, and the Java Depot brews a real caramel latte.

———⧜———

Q. In what 1986 movie sequel filmed at several Oregon locations does a cute dog befriend orphaned cougar cubs?

A. *Benji the Hunted.*

———⧜———

Q. In what 1989 made-for-television movie filmed in Portland does a woman race to stop a hit man before he can eliminate his next target?

A. *Dangerous Pursuit.*

———⧜———

Q. What is the seating capacity of the Arlene Schnitzer Concert Hall in Portland?

A. 2,776.

———⧜———

Q. Where can one see one of the finest natural history exhibits in the state?

A. Tillamook County Pioneer Museum in Tillamook.

HISTORY

Q. The Seth Thomas Model 17 clock on the Umatilla County Courthouse in Pendleton is one of how many such time-pieces built by the company?

A. Four.

Q. Why was a neon Rudolph the Red-Nosed Reindeer originally placed atop 1 Northwest Couch in Portland?

A. The neon deer was originally a logo for sportswear manufacturer White Stag.

Q. Who was John Day?

A. A member of the overland Astor-Hunt party of 1811–12, who with Ramsey Crooks fell behind the main party, was robbed by Indians and left naked at the mouth of the John Day River (both were found soon thereafter by Robert Stuart's company).

Q. What was a key factor in designating the gold rush town of Jacksonville as a National Historic Landmark Community?

A. Period photographs by Peter Britt that enabled accurate restoration of more than 90 original brick and wooden buildings dating back to the 1850s.

Q. What other Oregon attraction received a national designation partly as a result of Peter Britt's photographs?

A. Crater Lake, which was established as a National Park.

Q. How did the coastal Indians receive their first clues that other civilizations existed in the world?

A. From the wreckage of Spanish, Russian, and Chinese ships that washed ashore, introducing them to iron, copper, beeswax candles, and other manufactured goods.

Q. How did John Couch become the developer of Portland's first upscale residential district?

A. His family's land claim included prime locations in northwest Portland that Couch offered to thriving citizens of the booming town.

Q. Which Democratic presidential candidate successfully campaigned with the slogan "Fifty-four Forty or Fight"?

A. James K. Polk, in 1844 (the slogan refers to establishment of Oregon's northern border).

Q. French voyageurs once called the Columbia River by what name that is thought to be the source of the state's name?

A. Ouragan, meaning "hurricane."

Q. Before they founded Tektronix, Jack Murdock and Howard Vollum owned what business?

A. Murdock Radio and Appliance, a retail store on Foster Road in Portland.

Q. The beautiful four-place drinking fountains that can be found on several street corners in downtown Portland are called what?

A. Benson Bubblers.

———

Q. When did the Oregon Trail receive recognition as a National Historic Trail?

A. 1978.

———

Q. Who was first to ship lumber from Oregon?

A. Capt. John Meares, who harvested spars and otter furs in 1788–89 for his trip to China.

———

Q. What oceangoing vessel was storm-tossed onto the beach near Coos Bay in 1999?

A. *New Carissa.*

———

Q. Where was the 1904 Lewis and Clark Centennial Exposition sited?

A. Guild's Lake in northwest Portland.

———

Q. Public and private property damage resulting from the flood of 1996 amounted to how much?

A. $280 million for 27 affected counties.

———

Q. Pendleton's 57-foot courthouse clock cost how much in 1889?

A. $884.10 (its 1987–89 restoration cost more than $200,000).

Q. How many officials are elected in Oregon to manage state agencies?

A. Six: governor, secretary of state, treasurer, attorney general, commissioner of labor and industries, and superintendent of public instruction.

Q. What is Gov. John Kitzhaber's professional background?

A. Physician; he practiced emergency medicine and taught at Oregon Health Sciences University.

Q. How far up the Tualatin River did steamships travel before railroads were built?

A. Hillsboro.

Q. What was the origin of the eastern Oregon state park known as Kam Wah Chung?

A. A trading post that served the Chinese in John Day during the gold mining days of the 1850s.

Q. In 1883 how long did a train trip take between Saint Paul, Minnesota, and Portland?

A. Seven days, on the Northern Pacific Railroad.

Q. How much did it cost an immigrant to ride the Northern Pacific from Saint Paul to Portland in 1883?

A. $45, with sleeping cars available at no extra charge.

Q. What is purported to be buried at Neahkahnie Mountain?

A. A fortune in Spanish doubloons (carvings on beach rocks and ancient Indian legends are said to support the tale).

Q. Why did Simon Benson install his bubbling fountains in Portland?

A. To increase public sobriety by quenching loggers' thirst (he claimed saloon sales dropped 40 percent once the fountains were in operation).

Q. Until it burned in 1964, what was the sole surviving building of the Lewis and Clark Centennial Exposition?

A. Oregon Forestry Building, the world's largest log cabin.

Q. How did the White Stag company receive its name?

A. Originally sailmakers, the Hirsh-Weis company translated its German names into the English "white stag" when they began making sportswear.

Q. Who were the first European settlers in Oregon?

A. French-Canadian trappers retired from the Hudson's Bay Company who set up farms in the Saint Paul vicinity.

Q. Celilo Falls was obliterated in March 1957 by the body of water that formed behind what dam?

A. The Dalles.

Q. The address of Nike World Headquarters, One Bowerman Drive in Beaverton, was named for whom?

A. Bill Bowerman, track coach at the University of Oregon and a key member of the early Nike Corporation.

Q. Other than Oregon, what state does not allow self-service gasoline?

A. New Jersey.

Q. Prior to white settlement, Native Americans traveled to trade at Celilo from as far as what present-day Canadian province?

A. British Columbia.

Q. When did the nation's first pollution control laws go into effect?

A. 1938, when the State Sanitary Commission began cleaning up the Willamette and other Oregon waters.

Q. Who was the first man killed in Oregon while serving under American command?

A. Marcus Lopius, an African American who sailed with Robert Gray in 1788.

Q. What threat did Japan pose to Northwest forests during World War II?

A. Fire; balloons carrying incendiaries were sent aloft to drift over Oregon on the prevailing westerlies.

Q. How many Conestoga wagons traveled the Oregon Trail from 1840 to 1860?

A. None; they were too heavy for the western terrain.

Q. When was the battleship *Oregon* commissioned?

A. 1896; the vessel saw duty in the Spanish-American War but was obsolete by World War I.

Q. At the toll gate on the Santiam Pass Road in 1905, what fee was collected from the driver of the first car to cross the Cascade Mountains?

A. Three cents; a toll for cars had not yet been set, but frightened horses and livestock inspired the guard to establish the charge.

Q. How tall was the former Celilo Falls?

A. Eighty feet.

Q. Why is the office building at Portland's Northwest 27th and Vaughn Streets called Montgomery Park?

A. It originally was a Montgomery Ward warehouse, and only two letters in the roof sign needed to be changed for the new name.

Q. How many countries have consuls in Oregon?

A. Twenty-one: Barbados, Belgium, Czech Republic, Cyprus, Denmark, Finland, France, Germany, Great Britain, Ivory Coast, Japan, Korea, Malaysia, Mexico, Netherlands, Norway, Sweden, and Thailand (Mexico and the Netherlands also have consuls emeritus; Costa Rica, Lebanon, and Panama have consuls emeritus only).

Q. Who was Capt. George Flavel?

A. A Columbia River bar pilot and Astoria's first millionaire, whose 1885 Victorian mansion in Astoria is open to the public.

Q. How many Benson Bubblers are in downtown Portland?

A. Forty.

Q. Who was the first provisional governor of the Oregon Territory?

A. George Abernathy, for whom Abernathy Green, the terminus of the Oregon Trail, is named.

Q. How did the news of Oregon's statehood reach Portland on March 15, 1859?

A. Aboard the ship *Brother Jonathan*.

Q. How many shipwrecks are near the mouth of the Columbia River?

A. More than 2,000 have been documented.

Q. Which two Portland mayors served four terms?

A. Terry Shrunk (1956–1972) and George L. Baker (1917–1933).

Q. Who was the biggest promoter of Portland's eastside MAX Light Rail Line?

A. Mayor Neil Goldschmidt.

Q. What was the original construction cost of the Columbia River Highway from Astoria to The Dalles?

A. $11 million.

———∞∞∞———

Q. In the late 18th century, why did Boston merchants want sea otter pelts from the Northwest coast?

A. To trade with China for tea, silk, and other Asian goods that were in high demand in Boston (China eschewed New England trade goods but wanted otter pelts).

———∞∞∞———

Q. In numerical order of admittance to the Union, what is Oregon's position?

A. Thirty-third.

———∞∞∞———

Q. How much of Oregon's rail traffic originates in the state?

A. Approximately 57 percent (8 million of an estimated 14 million tons annually).

———∞∞∞———

Q. What enabled the Oregon Steam Navigation Company to make a return of $783,339 on an investment of $172,500 in just four years?

A. Discovery of gold in Idaho and Eastern Oregon, which led thousands of people to seek passage up the Columbia River.

———∞∞∞———

Q. What U.S. government post did Neil Goldschmidt hold after serving as mayor of Portland?

A. Secretary of transportation under Jimmy Carter.

Q. In 1872 how did "Oregon Swamp Rat" Henry Owen convince the land board that the property he had purchased was low-value swamp land?

A. He put a rowboat on his wagon and later swore that he had thoroughly inspected the site "in a boat."

———⊗⊗⊗———

Q. Why did the pioneers of Tillamook build the schooner *Morning Star*?

A. To take their dairy products and farm crops to market (no captains outside the area dared enter Tillamook Bay due to the danger of crossing the bar).

———⊗⊗⊗———

Q. What early explorer's journals discouraged other captains from visiting "New Albion," as he called the Pacific Northwest?

A. Sir Francis Drake, who ransacked the Spanish fleet and then fled to the Oregon coast, where he experienced rough weather in June 1579.

———⊗⊗⊗———

Q. When was the present state capitol building rebuilt?

A. 1938, following a fire in 1935.

———⊗⊗⊗———

Q. Who was the first citizen of Tillamook?

A. Joe Champion, who lived in a hollow tree, then served as the first county clerk and taught in the town's first school.

———⊗⊗⊗———

Q. What early 20th-century shipwreck can visitors to Fort Stevens see on the beach?

A. *Peter Iredale.*

Q. How could new immigrants fresh off the Oregon Trail be distinguished from those already settled in the Willamette Valley?

A. New settlers were said to be better dressed, while older settlers were better fed.

Q. Who was Oregon's first governor?

A. Peter Burnett.

Q. What renowned manufacturer of wool shirts and blankets takes its name from the city in which its first plant opened?

A. Pendleton Woolen Mills.

Q. What major benefit did Oregon derive from the California gold rush?

A. A large, nearby market for its produce and grain.

Q. Why did Spain relinquish its claim to sovereignty over Oregon in 1819?

A. The Treaty of Florida gave Texas to Spain in return for ceding Oregon claims at 42 degrees north latitude (the present southern border of the state) to the United States.

Q. How many people traveled the Oregon Trail between 1840 and 1860?

A. More than 53,000.

Q. Who is alleged to have said on surrendering to the U.S. Cavalry, "From where the sun now stands, I will fight no more forever?"

A. Chief Joseph of the Nez Percé.

Q. In 1883 what travel concessions did the Northern Pacific Railroad make to immigrant groups?

A. It allowed groups of 30 or more who bought their tickets at the same time to have a coach reserved for their use.

Q. Why were Portland's original city blocks laid out in 60-by-200-foot spaces?

A. The plan, called a "dollhouse plat," maximized available corner lots.

Q. What was the first steamboat on the Willamette River?

A. *Lot Whitcomb,* built in 1850 at Milwaukie.

Q. The city of Pendleton was named after what Ohio vice presidential candidate in 1864?

A. George Hunt Pendleton, whose Oregon relative proposed his name.

Q. What reference did Don Estevan Martinez use on his voyage to proclaim sovereignty over Oregon for the king of Spain?

A. A copy of the map Capt. James Cook made while sailing along the Oregon coast in 1778 and later published in London.

Q. What drove California cattlemen in the late 19th century to purchase ranches in Oregon's high desert country?

A. California's Fence Laws. (The cattlemen sought open range lands.)

Q. Prior to Lewis and Clark's Corps of Discovery in 1804-1806, what three other countries contested with the United States for dominion over the Oregon Country?

A. Spain, England, and Russia.

Q. How much was the only toll ever imposed on U.S. 99 between Mexico and Canada?

A. Twenty-five cents, levied in 1960 on the Interstate Bridge linking Portland with Vancouver, Washington.

Q. Which U.S. senator from Oregon first advised the nation of the inadvisability of an American commitment to the Republic of Vietnam?

A. Wayne L. Morse.

Q. Where was gold first discovered in the Oregon Territory?

A. Rich Gulch, in 1851.

Q. Claire Munson became the first woman to be elected mayor of a town in the West when the citizens of what community voted her into office in 1913?

A. Warrenton.

Q. How soon after gold was discovered did Jacksonville come alive with saloons, gambling halls, supply stores, and various other enterprises?

A. Within a year, by winter 1852.

Q. Who was the first woman to be elected mayor of Portland?

A. Dorothy McCullough Lee, in 1949 (she was also the second woman elected mayor of a major U.S. metropolis, following Seattle in 1924).

Q. Who were the first Europeans known to have stood on the soil of the Northwest?

A. Bruno Heceta and Juan Francisco de Bodega y Quadra.

Q. When did the Portland police start using radios?

A. 1934, becoming the first police agency in the nation to do so.

Q. Who was the first man to drive cattle from California to Oregon?

A. Ewing Young, in the 1830s.

Q. What U.S. president spent five of his childhood years in Newberg?

A. Herbert Hoover, who lived with his aunt and uncle, Laura Ellen Miles and Dr. Henry John Minthorn.

Q. In the late 19th century, what successful company ran steamboats up to the gold mines of Idaho, eastern Washington, and western Montana?

A. Oregon Steam Navigation Company.

Q. What careers did John Minthorn follow?

A. Superintendent of the Indian Manual Training School and, in 1884, head of Pacific Academy (later George Fox College).

Q. Fort Yamhill, an authentic 1856 military blockhouse, stands in the courthouse square of what town?

A. Dayton (the structure was moved there in 1911).

Q. What Oregon city was once named capital of the United States?

A. Meacham, proclaimed the nation's honorary capital for one day by President Warren G. Harding to acknowledge completion of U.S. 40, the first transcontinental highway.

Q. The Multnomah County portion of the Columbia River Highway became the first major paved highway in the Pacific Northwest in what year?

A. 1916.

Q. Who was the first woman appointed police chief of a major U.S. city?

A. Penny Harrington, 1985 in Portland.

Q. For whom was Reed College named in 1910?

A. Simeon and Amanda Reed, who owned the Oregon Steam Navigation Company.

Q. What was often referred to as the nation's largest housing project?

A. Vanport, south of Jantzen Beach, which had 18,700 tenants in 1948 and was originally constructed to house workers building liberty ships.

Q. The fur of what Oregon animal was traded first?

A. Sea otter.

Q. Who was the first European to cross the North American continent to the Pacific Ocean?

A. Sir Alexander MacKenzie, in 1793.

Q. What experience made Abigail Scott Duniway increasingly aware of unequal treatment of men and women by the law?

A. Operating a women's hat shop in Albany.

Q. Who is known as the "Father of Oregon"?

A. John McLoughlin.

Q. Which two captains arrived at the mouth of the Columbia River in 1792?

A. Robert Gray and George Vancouver (on separate trips).

Q. What are Century Farms?

A. Oregon farms under the same family's ownership for at least 100 years.

⊸⊸⊸

Q. When did crews stop manning the Tillamook Rock lighthouse?

A. 1957.

⊸⊸⊸

Q. Who was the first white man to travel the entire length of the Columbia River?

A. David Thompson, who worked for Canada's North West Company from 1797 to 1812.

⊸⊸⊸

Q. Who was the first woman admitted to the Oregon Bar Association?

A. Mary Leonard, in 1886, seven years after being acquitted of killing her husband.

⊸⊸⊸

Q. What was known in 1902 as the "Oregon System"?

A. The nation's first initiative, referendum, and repeal laws, which allowed citizens to enact and repeal legislation and remove undesirable officials from office.

⊸⊸⊸

Q. In 1908, when gill netters and fish wheelers both filed initiatives outlawing the other's practices, what was the result?

A. Voters outlawed both methods of commercial fishing.

Q. What role did U.S. Navy Lt. William Slacum play in Oregon history?

A. He broke the Hudson's Bay Company monopoly on cattle by persuading settlers to buy California cattle.

Q. In 1843 settlers organized a provisional government based on the laws of what state?

A. Iowa.

Q. Marking the beginning of the consumer protection movement, who was appointed Portland's city market inspector in 1905?

A. Sarah A. Evans, the first such inspector appointed in the U.S.

Q. In 1819 a treaty between the United States and what country fixed the present southern boundary of Oregon?

A. Spain.

Q. The United States and Great Britain in 1818 reached what agreement concerning the Oregon region?

A. A joint occupancy treaty that permitted citizens of both countries to settle and trade there.

Q. What was the mission of Meriwether Lewis and William Clark?

A. To explore and map the Louisiana Purchase lands and lay claim to the Oregon region for the United States.

Q. What was the name of the guide Lewis and Clark met in North Dakota who led the Corps of Discovery to the Pacific Ocean?

A. Sacajawea, a Shoshone woman.

———⊗⊗⊗———

Q. Who was Concomly?

A. A chief of the Chinooks in what is now Clatsop County.

———⊗⊗⊗———

Q. What company was formed by early Oregon settlers to buy California cows?

A. Willamette Cattle Company.

———⊗⊗⊗———

Q. The National Capitol Rotunda features a statue of what early U.S. senator from Oregon?

A. Col. Edward D. Baker, a close friend of Abraham Lincoln.

———⊗⊗⊗———

Q. What crucial food supply served a dual purpose for settlers who traveled the Oregon Trail?

A. Wheat, used for food and for planting in the new land.

———⊗⊗⊗———

Q. Who were Oregon's first U.S. senators after statehood?

A. Joseph Lane and Delazon Smith.

———⊗⊗⊗———

Q. When did the transcontinental telegraph reach Portland?

A. 1864.

Q. In the 1880s and 1890s, what two Oregonians designed and manufactured a steam-driven riverboat to tow logs to sawmills?

A. Nathaniel P. Slate of Tangent and Daniel Best, an Albany machine shop patternmaker.

Q. How long did it take pioneers to complete a journey on the 2,000-mile-long Oregon Trail?

A. Six to eight months.

Q. Who supplied immigrants to Oregon City with food, clothing, temporary shelter, and even jobs?

A. John McLoughlin, director of the Hudson's Bay Company and "ruler" of the region for 20 years.

Q. Before the arrival of the Europeans and Americans, what habitat did the Coastal Indians use?

A. Plank houses.

Q. After sighting the Pacific Ocean in 1805, Lewis and Clark built what shelter near present-day Astoria?

A. Fort Clatsop.

Q. When was Corvallis College founded?

A. 1868, by the Methodist Church (it later became Oregon State University).

Q. What thoroughfare enabled Portland shippers to receive produce that was sent to miners during the California gold rush?

A. Canyon Road.

Q. In 1959 who established the Century Farm Program for Oregon's Centennial of Statehood?

A. Oregon Historical Society.

———

Q. When did Portland first receive transcontinental railroad service?

A. 1883.

———

Q. What happened to Astoria as a result of the 1818 joint occupancy treaty between the U.S. and Great Britain?

A. It returned to American ownership.

———

Q. How did Henry Pittock, longtime editor of *The Oregonian,* and his wife, Georgiana, get to Oregon?

A. They traveled the Oregon Trail, in the 1850s.

———

Q. What was the childhood home of Gov. Tom McCall, who served 1967–1975?

A. Westernworld Ranch, near Redmond.

———

Q. What legislation passed in 1929 marked the beginning of environmental law?

A. Oregon Reforestation Act, requiring that timber companies replant logged-out areas.

———

Q. When was the bridge that currently spans Alsea Bay at Waldport built?

A. 1991 (the first bridge there was constructed in 1936).

Q. Who most commonly named towns in Oregon?

A. Local postmasters.

———— ⬡ ————

Q. Who founded the Pacific Fur Company?

A. John Jacob Astor.

———— ⬡ ————

Q. At the height of rail travel, how many trains arrived and departed Portland's Union Station each day?

A. Seventy-four.

———— ⬡ ————

Q. What was the name of the first steamboat on the Pacific Ocean?

A. *Beaver.*

———— ⬡ ————

Q. What East Coast fashion was especially responsible for the Northwest fur trade?

A. Beaver hats.

———— ⬡ ————

Q. Where did Henry Villard originally envision the site of Portland's railroad station?

A. On the east side of the North Park blocks, possibly near where the U.S. Customs House stands today.

———— ⬡ ————

Q. When was daily stagecoach service initiated between Sacramento and Portland?

A. 1860.

Q. Where were some of the early exhibits of the Oregon Museum of Science and Industry displayed?

A. Portland City Hall (beginning in 1906) and the Portland Hotel and two local banks (beginning in 1944).

———∞———

Q. When did the United States and Great Britain agree to the 49th parallel as the northern boundary of the Oregon region?

A. 1846.

———∞———

Q. Who was Jane Barnes?

A. The first woman of European stock born in Oregon (1814).

———∞———

Q. Who was Oregon's first woman governor?

A. Barbara Roberts (1991–1995).

———∞———

Q. What name did Lewis and Clark give the Willamette River?

A. Multnomah.

———∞———

Q. When did Oregon sawmills begin shipping lumber to China?

A. 1833.

———∞———

Q. What Ohio man walked the Oregon Trail in 1849 and later served as an Oregon district court judge for 33 years?

A. Matthew Deady.

Q. When the Portland Police Department was founded in 1851, how were policemen paid?

A. From fines and fees for services provided (salaries were established in 1868).

Q. What is considered one of the worst floods in Oregon history in terms of volume of floodwaters?

A. The flood of 1861, which wiped out Champoeg.

Q. How much prime timber was destroyed in the Tillamook burn of 1933?

A. About 240,000 acres.

Q. What was the name of the first Oregonian of Chinese ancestry?

A. Sung Sung (1851).

Q. What town grew up around a pool table that was destined for a mining camp, fell off its wagon and couldn't be reloaded?

A. Kerby.

Q. Who envisioned a "great metropolis" at the juncture of the Willamette and Columbia Rivers?

A. Hall J. Kelley, a Bostonian who did much to promote emigration to Oregon.

Q. How many Oregonians were killed in action in the Vietnam War?

A. 751.

Q. What tools did the Coastal Indians use to make planks for their houses?

A. Wedges made from elk horn, bone, or yew wood (to split cedar and redwood drift logs) and stone adzes (used to trim the resulting boards).

Q. What was the first legislation in the nation to encourage recycling by giving refunds for glass and aluminum products?

A. Oregon Bottle Bill, enacted in 1971.

Q. By 1985 how many other states had enacted recycling legislation?

A. Nine.

Q. For what crime was one Mr. Travolet, the first occupant of the Portland Jail, arrested?

A. For "riding at a furious rate" through the city.

Q. What Methodist missionary founded Salem in 1841?

A. Jason Lee.

Q. According to the 1850 census, how many people lived in Oregon?

A. 12,093.

Q. Who was the first child born to settlers in the Oregon country?

A. Alice Clarrisa Whitman, daughter of Marcus and Narcissa Whitman (1836).

Q. What Champoeg resident aided victims of the 1861 flood, despite sustaining great financial losses himself?

A. Robert Newell, whose house was on higher ground.

———— ∞∞∞ ————

Q. In 1847 what did new settlers bring to the Oregon country that dramatically reduced the Native American population?

A. Measles epidemic.

———— ∞∞∞ ————

Q. In what year did a U.S. census first count more than 100,000 people in Oregon?

A. 1880.

———— ∞∞∞ ————

Q. Where did Jason Lee establish a school for Native American children in 1834?

A. French Prairie.

———— ∞∞∞ ————

Q. Who founded Oregon City?

A. John McLoughlin, in 1842.

———— ∞∞∞ ————

Q. Named for Hall J. Kelley, where is Kelley Point located?

A. At the juncture of the Willamette and Columbia Rivers.

———— ∞∞∞ ————

Q. What led to the formation of Oregon's first government in 1843?

A. "Wolf Meetings," which were called to tackle problems associated with wild animals.

Q. The bill to establish a state constitution went before the legislature four times before it was approved by how large a margin?

A. Two votes, 52–50.

Q. When did Oregon become territory?

A. 1848.

Q. When were Oregon's present boundaries established?

A. 1853, when Congress created the Washington Territory.

Q. What feature can be seen on all the doorknobs in the state capitol?

A. Oregon State Seal.

Q. What Presbyterian missionaries were massacred by the Native Americans they served?

A. Dr. Marcus and Narcissa Whitman, in 1847.

Q. From 1845 to 1851 which fledgling cities on the Willamette River strove to be the primary port serving the entire area?

A. Oregon City, Portland, Milwaukie, and Saint Helens.

Q. How much did first-class postage cost when the Oregon Territory's first post office opened in Astoria on May 9, 1847?

A. Forty cents.

Q. What is the oldest institution of higher learning west of Missouri?

A. Willamette University, founded in 1842 as the Oregon Institute.

———⊗⊗⊗———

Q. How old was John Corbin Barnum when he began his railroad career with the Rogue River Valley Railway?

A. Twelve (he later became general manager).

———⊗⊗⊗———

Q. When did the Port of Portland start dredging the Willamette River to a depth of 25 feet?

A. 1891.

———⊗⊗⊗———

Q. Who was the first Japanese settler to arrive in Oregon?

A. Miyo Iwakoshi, in 1880.

———⊗⊗⊗———

Q. What governor declared Oregon beaches to be state highways?

A. Oswald West, in 1913.

———⊗⊗⊗———

Q. On what date did Oregon become a state?

A. February 14, 1859.

———⊗⊗⊗———

Q. When did Portland's first Morrison Bridge replace the Stark Street Ferry?

A. April 12, 1887 (it was the first bridge across the Willamette and the longest span west of the Mississippi).

Q. Who was the first African American to settle in Oregon?

A. George Washington Bush, in 1851.

Q. When did the Northern Pacific Railway begin offering transcontinental rail service to Oregon's largest city?

A. September 4, 1883.

Q. What state agency established in 1921 served as a model for those in other states?

A. Oregon State Board of Aeronautics, regulating fliers and flying.

Q. How many covered bridges were built in Oregon?

A. About 300.

Q. What was unique about Portland's Mass Transit Mall when it opened in May 1978?

A. It was the first in the U.S. to have one-way streets.

Q. What bridge's 6,000-ton mid span, representing 10 times more weight than had ever been lifted previously, was hydraulically raised 170 feet into place in 1973?

A. Portland's Fremont Bridge.

Q. In 1893 Erickson's Saloon in Portland was said to have the "world's longest bar" at how many feet?

A. 684 (the bar was horseshoe-shaped and serviced by 50 bartenders).

Q. During the 1906 election, Oregon voters became the first in the nation to do what?

A. Elect U.S. senators directly (in other states, senators were elected by state legislators until 1913).

Q. What is the only American city to remove a complete freeway from its downtown area?

A. Portland.

Q. Where was U.S. Senator and former Oregon governor Mark O. Hatfield born?

A. Dallas, Oregon, July 12, 1922.

Q. Who were the Rajneeshees?

A. Followers of a guru from India who bought the Big Muddy ranch outside Antelope (1981–85) and changed the name of the town to Rajneesh.

Q. What attorney was a driving force in associating Portland with roses?

A. Frederick V. Holman, founder of the Portland Rose Society in 1888 and a prime mover behind the city's first Rose Festival in 1907.

Q. What evidence of the Oswego Iron Works' existence can still be seen today?

A. Many of the iron-front buildings that remain in Portland (and some in San Francisco) were manufactured by the company, and a 25-foot-tall blast-furnace base can be seen at George Rogers Park in Lake Oswego.

Q. On what date did Mt. St. Helens erupt, covering the Portland area in volcanic ash?

A. May 18, 1980.

———⊗⊗⊘———

Q. Prior to Tom McCall Waterfront Park, what occupied the west bank of the Willamette in Oregon's largest city?

A. A freeway.

———⊗⊗⊘———

Q. According to myths of Native Americans in the Northwest, what helped God in the creation of the world?

A. Beavers.

———⊗⊗⊘———

Q. What purpose did Ashland's Winchester Inn initially serve?

A. The building, located on East Main Street on the present-day site of the Columbia Hotel, housed the Southern Oregon Hospital.

———⊗⊗⊘———

Q. According to the document's preamble, why did the people of Oregon ordain the state constitution?

A. To see "justice established, order maintained, and liberty perpetuated."

———⊗⊗⊘———

Q. What is the first Article of the Oregon Constitution?

A. Bill of Rights.

———⊗⊗⊘———

Q. Where can one find the birthplace of Earl Snell, Oregon governor from 1942 to 1947?

A. Olex, in Gilliam County.

ARTS & LITERATURE

C H A P T E R F O U R

Q. In 1822 who made the first American use of the name "Origon" when he urged Congress to encourage settlement of the territory?

A. Dr. John Floyd.

Q. Where was Portland's first symphony concert conducted?

A. Oro Fino Hall, June 15, 1866.

Q. How many Oregon newspapers have won a Pulitzer Prize?

A. Two: *Medford Mail Tribune* (1934) and *The Oregonian* (1939 and 1954).

Q. Where is the world-class Oregon Bach Festival held?

A. University of Oregon, Eugene.

Q. Where did composer Ernest Bloch live?

A. Agate Beach.

Q. Who presents the C. E. S. Wood Retrospective for a distinguished career in Oregon letters and the Stewart H. Holbrook Special Award for contributions to Oregon literary life?

A. Literary Arts, Inc.

Q. When was the Portland Art Association founded?

A. 1892.

Q. What Oregonian wrote *Winterkill, Riversong,* and *Sky Fisherman*?

A. Craig Lesley.

Q. For what work did Portland's William Stafford win the National Book Award in 1963?

A. *Traveling Through the Dark.*

Q. Called the "Buffalo Bill of American Literature," what colorful 19th-century Oregon-based poet wrote *My Life among the Modocs*?

A. Joaquin Miller.

Q. Who wrote *Marooned at Crater Lake* and *History of Oregon Literature*?

A. Alfred Powers.

Q. Which onetime member of the band Paul Revere and the Raiders now writes whodunnits?

A. Pierre Oulette, a partner in Portland advertising firm KVO.

Q. What public event in Ashland preceded the Oregon Shakespeare Festival there?

A. Chautauqua.

———oooo———

Q. Who received the National Book Award for his book *Arctic Dreams*?

A. Barry Lopez.

———oooo———

Q. When Oregon State graduated its first class in 1870, how many women received degrees?

A. One (out of a class of three).

———oooo———

Q. What do titles such as *Undaunted Courage, From Sea to Shining Sea, Bold Journey, Forward the Nation,* and *Two Captains West* have in common?

A. They chronicle the explorations of Lewis and Clark.

———oooo———

Q. Who sculpted the statue *Oregon Pioneer* that stands atop the rotunda of the state capitol?

A. Ulric Ellerhausen.

———oooo———

Q. What is the most ancient work of art at Portland City Hall?

A. A 16th-century petroglyph displayed in the east courtyard.

———oooo———

Q. In 1987 the Oregon Historical Society published a translation of *Oregon East, Oregon West,* written in 1874 for a German audience by what author?

A. Theodor Kirchoff.

Q. What Oregon author began his book *River Why* by comparing a baby in the womb with a fish in a snug little river?

A. David James Duncan.

———∞∞———

Q. Who was named Oregon's poet laureate in 1975?

A. William Stafford.

———∞∞———

Q. Computer guru Steve Jobs is an alumnus of what Oregon college?

A. Reed.

———∞∞———

Q. What Astoria native born in 1824 defied rules against foreigners and tutored 14 Japanese in the English language, the first to do so on Japanese soil?

A. Ranald McDonald.

———∞∞———

Q. How tall is the statue *Oregon Pioneer* at the state capitol?

A. Twenty-four feet, weighing 8.5 tons.

———∞∞———

Q. What genres is author Ursula K. Le Guin best known for?

A. Science-fiction and fantasy.

———∞∞———

Q. By what nickname do Portlanders affectionately call their concert hall?

A. "The Schnitz" (Arlene Schnitzer Concert Hall).

Q. What did David James Duncan call his father in *River Why*?

A. H2O.

———⊗———

Q. According to legends of the Coos tribe, why does skunk cabbage grow sheathed in a yellow cloak?

A. As a reward for being a necessary food supply in the early spring.

———⊗———

Q. What photographer has produced such albums as *Oregon, Oregon II, Oregon III,* and *Beautiful Oregon*?

A. Ray Atkeson.

———⊗———

Q. What mother of a governor described the rigors of ranch life near Prineville in her autobiography, *Ranch under the Rimrock*?

A. Dorothy Lawson McCall.

———⊗———

Q. In Ken Kesey's *One Flew Over the Cuckoo's Nest,* what did Chief want to see once he escaped from the psychiatric ward?

A. Indians fishing from traditional fish scaffolding attached to hydroelectric dams on the Columbia River.

———⊗———

Q. At the Chinatown gate at Fourth and Burnside in Portland, what objects are the dragons holding?

A. One holds a ball, the other a young dragon.

———⊗———

Q. Why does Portland have few buildings built prior to 1872?

A. Much of the city was destroyed by fire that year.

Q. How many varieties of roses are in the International Rose Test Garden at Portland's Washington Park?

A. Approximately 400.

Q. Stephen Ambrose wrote what book about the Lewis and Clark Expedition?

A. *Undaunted Courage.*

Q. Where is Portland's Glazed Terra Cotta District?

A. Southwest Fifth and Sixth Avenues between Oak and Yamhill Streets.

Q. Who stated, "I am throwing myself at you. I want to play with that wonderful company of yours and it won't cost you a cent."?

A. Actor Charles Laughton in a letter to the founder of the Oregon Shakespeare Company.

Q. What is the only Oregon college classified as a Carnegie Research I institution?

A. Oregon State University.

Q. What director of the Northwest Writing Institute at Lewis and Clark College wrote *The Granary, A Gypsy's History of the World,* and *Having Everything Right: Essays of Place.*

A. Kim Stafford.

Q. When was the Oregon Shakespeare Festival established?

A. 1935.

Q. In 1997, what orchestra had the highest paid subscription attendance per capita of any orchestra in the nation?

A. Oregon Symphony.

Q. Where was noted children's author Beverly Cleary born?

A. McMinnville, in 1916.

Q. Opal Whitely recounted her experiences as a child growing up in Walden, near Cottage Grove in the Cascade Mountains, in what book?

A. Her juvenile diary, which caused a sensation when it was serialized in *Atlantic Monthly* in 1923 as *Opal, the Journal of an Understanding Heart.*

Q. What house may have been the inspiration for the Stamper house in Ken Kesey's *Sometimes a Great Notion?*

A. Benedict house on Cox Island, near Florence.

Q. What Southern Oregon Normal School faculty member brought live theater to the town of Ashland and the college there in 1931?

A. Angus L. Bowmer.

Q. From what Oregon college did former White House intern Monica Lewinsky graduate?

A. Lewis and Clark.

Q. Who wrote newspaper columns, feature articles, and several books on logging?

A. Curt Beckham (1908–1990).

———— ∞ ————

Q. In what apocalyptic novel by Ursula K. LeGuin did the snow melt off Mount Hood?

A. *The Lathe of Heaven.*

———— ∞ ————

Q. How did Henry Pittock become publisher of *The Oregonian*?

A. He received the paper in lieu of back wages when owner Thomas J. Dryer was appointed U.S. commissioner of the Sandwich Islands (Hawaii) by Abraham Lincoln.

———— ∞ ————

Q. Noting extreme gloominess among the inhabitants of Portland, German author Theodor Kirchoff offered what explanation?

A. He said they loved the overcast skies and rain so much that the sight of the sun made them unhappy.

———— ∞ ————

Q. In Bernard Malumud's *A New Life,* the town of Eastchester, Cascadia, is a fictionized rendition of what Oregon town?

A. Corvallis.

———— ∞ ————

Q. What is the name of the private detective who drives a Jaguar XK-E in the novels of Oregon author M. K. Wren?

A. Conan Flag.

Q. Who, on visiting foggy San Francisco, said to his guide, "In Fort Rock, [Oregon] we don't have bridges, islands, or harbors at all, but if we had 'em, we could see 'em."

A. Reub Long, in the novel *The Oregon Desert.*

———◆———

Q. How many theaters does the Oregon Shakespeare Festival operate in Ashland?

A. Three.

———◆———

Q. What was the first major hammered-copper sculpture to be commissioned since the Statue of Liberty?

A. *Portlandia,* erected in 1985 above the Fifth Avenue entrance to the Portland Building.

———◆———

Q. Whose literary memoirs published in 1984 were titled *Assault on Mount Helicon?*

A. Oregon author and poet Mary Barnard.

———◆———

Q. What professor of anthropology at the University of Oregon wrote *Prehistory of the Far West* and discovered 10,000-year-old sandals at Fort Rock Cave?

A. Luther S. Cressman.

———◆———

Q. What educational outreach program does the Oregon Shakespeare Festival offer?

A. Annual performances before 137,000 students in 254 schools throughout the Far West, Alaska, and Hawaii.

Q. Who wrote "Fish-Hawk and Other Heroes"?

A. Jarold Ramsey.

Q. Along with 13 of his graduate students in creative writing, Ken Kesey wrote a mystery novel, *Caverns,* under what joint pseudonym?

A. O. U. Levon, which read backwards is "novel U. O. (University of Oregon)."

Q. What poet and English professor at Portland State University penned *Love Is Not a Consolation; It Is a Light?*

A. Primus St. John.

Q. Who wrote *Moontrap, To Build a Ship, Mountain Men: The Trappers of the Fur Trade,* and *Trask?*

A. Tillamook author Don Berry.

Q. For which book did Ursula K. Le Guin win the National Book Award?

A. *The Farthest Shore* (1972).

Q. What Oregon musical ensemble can boast that its members have performed with the New York Philharmonic, Chicago Symphony, Los Angeles Philharmonic, San Francisco Symphony, Boston Symphony, and the Philadelphia Orchestra?

A. Oregon Coast Music Festival Orchestra of Coos Bay.

Q. Where might one attend an "off-Bardway" play?

A. Ashland, at the Oregon Shakespeare Festival.

───⊗───

Q. What Portland lawyer wrote *The Last Innocent Man, The Burning Man,* and *After Dark?*

A. Phillip Margolin.

───⊗───

Q. What was the first piece of public art commissioned in Portland?

A. Skidmore Fountain, in 1886.

───⊗───

Q. Under construction from 1913 to 1922, what is known as the "Poem in Stone"?

A. Columbia River Highway.

───⊗───

Q. Who wrote *Stepping Westward: The Long Search for Home in the Pacific Northwest* and *The Sorcerers Apprentice?*

A. Sally Tisdale.

───⊗───

Q. In 1896 the first symphony orchestra west of the Mississippi was conducted by whom?

A. W. H. Kinross, in Portland.

───⊗───

Q. How did Jean Auel, who lives on the Oregon coast, research her 1980 bestseller, *The Clan of the Cave Bear?*

A. By attending an outdoor survival school.

Q. Oregonian H. L. Davis received a Pulitzer Prize for what novel?

A. *Honey in the Horn.*

Q. Gov. Tom McCall issued what unusual invitation to tourists?

A. "Visit as often as you like, but don't come here to live."

Q. How long does the Oregon Shakespeare Festival season run?

A. Eight months, mid-February through October.

Q. What trade group formed the first labor union in Oregon?

A. Typographical Society.

Q. Ramona Quimby is a character created by what Oregon author?

A. Beverly Cleary.

Q. According to Jarold Ramsey, what were the three most popular books in central Oregon in the early 20th century?

A. The Bible and the "Sears and Sawbucks" and "Monkey Ward" catalogs.

Q. What author who resides in eastern Oregon wrote *Don Coyote*?

A. Dayton Ogden Hyde, in 1986.

Q. What was the first newspaper published in Oregon?

A. *The Oregon Spectator,* in Oregon City (1846).

Q. Where was Washington County's first school?

A. Hillsboro, in a one-room log cabin.

Q. Raised in Warner Valley, what author wrote *Owning It All* and *We Are Not in This Together*?

A. William Kittridge.

Q. When did the Portland Symphony Orchestra change its name to the Oregon Symphony?

A. 1993 (it was known as the Oregon Symphony Orchestra from 1967 until 1993).

Q. Besides attending Harvard and the University of Oregon, Erskine Wood, eldest son of C. E. S. Wood, had what unique element in his education?

A. He lived with Chief Joseph of the Nez Percé.

Q. How did the Wood family become acquainted with Chief Joseph?

A. In 1879 C. E. S. Wood was a first lieutenant in the army's campaigns against the Nez Percé.

Q. What noted author claimed that Portland has such a low-key approach to celebrity that "being a celebrity is such a waste of time"?

A. Ursula K. Le Guin.

Q. Who was the first man to reach Oregon and leave a written account?

A. Bartolome Ferrelo, pilot for Juan Rodriguez Cabrillo.

Q. In the 1920s what reporter for the *Oregon Journal* wrote a number of books on the Oregon Trail and pioneer days?

A. Fred Lockley, the "Journal Man."

Q. In 1988 George Venn and Ulrich H. Hardt compiled what series of books at the suggestion of the Oregon Council of Teachers of English?

A. *Oregon Literature,* in six volumes.

Q. According to author Don Berry in *Mountain Men: The Trappers of the Fur Trade Era,* what was the heritage of Chief Kilchi?

A. He was a descendent of a black shipwreck survivor in the Tillamook country.

Q. A $5,000 bequest was given to Portland in 1888 to build what place where "horses, men, and dogs could drink"?

A. Skidmore Fountain.

Q. Who wrote *The River of the West,* a biography of mountain man Joe Meek?

A. Frances Fuller Victor.

Q. What Portlander wrote many Westerns, including *The Earthbreakers*?

A. Earnest Haycox.

———————

Q. Whose diary sat in an attic bureau drawer for 60 years until his daughter had it published in 1962, as *The Golden Frontier*?

A. Herman Francis Reinhart (1832–1889).

———————

Q. What Oregon attorney printed *1601* for Mark Twain?

A. C. E. S. Wood (the small print run now makes it a rare book).

———————

Q. What Boston writer praised the merits of Oregon although he had not been there?

A. Hall J. Kelley (later, in the 1840s, he did visit the state).

———————

Q. What was the theme of *The Begum's Fortune,* a novel by Jules Verne set in Oregon and as yet not translated into English?

A. The ability of technology to enhance or destroy nature.

———————

Q. Which of her novels did Ursula K. Le Guin dedicate to her mother, Theodora?

A. *Tombs of Atuan,* published in 1971.

———————

Q. Bankers honored the checks of what rancher, even though they were written on soup can labels and shingles?

A. Bill Brown, of Lake and Crook Counties.

Q. What 1983 book did the *Houston Post* compare to *Zen and the Art of Motorcycle Maintenance* and *Catch 22*?

A. *River Why* by David James Duncan.

———⊗⊗⊗———

Q. What entrepreneur who controlled 94,095 acres of land along the Rogue River, effectively owning the tidewater salmon fishery there, penned *Salmon of the Pacific Coast*?

A. Robert Deniston Hume (1845–1908).

———⊗⊗⊗———

Q. What noted American author wrote *Astoria* in 1836 to report on John Jacob Astor's fur trading business in Oregon?

A. Washington Irving.

———⊗⊗⊗———

Q. What national news magazine in 1977 said of Oregon, "[T]his state of scenic grandeur and easygoing individualism is writing the preface to what may be the future for all Americans: simple living, conservation and limited growth"?

A. *U.S. News and World Report.*

———⊗⊗⊗———

Q. *Wildmen, Wobblies & Whistle Punks* is an anthology of whose work?

A. Stewart Holbrook (1893–1964).

———⊗⊗⊗———

Q. What are the names of the Shakespeare Festival theaters in Ashland?

A. Elizabethan Stage (opened in 1935), Angus Bowmer Theater (1970), and Black Swan (1977).

Q. In 1933–34 what Native American woman dictated oral traditions and songs of the Miluuk and Coos Indians to Melville Jacobs of the University of Washington?

A. Annie Miner Peterson, one of the last Coos raised in the old traditions.

———∞———

Q. What American university in 1993 began offering a second, concurrent bachelor's degree in international studies in any major offered on campus?

A. Oregon State University.

———∞———

Q. What book by Ursula K. Le Guin earned her the *Boston Globe*-Horn Book Award in 1968, the Lewis Carroll Shelf Award in 1979, and the Horn Book honor list citation?

A. *A Wizard of Earthsea.*

———∞———

Q. Who founded the Oregon Institute for Literary Arts?

A. Brian Booth.

———∞———

Q. How did Jesse Winburne, donor of Ashland's Lithia Park, make his fortune?

A. Advertising.

———∞———

Q. What modern poet is known for his promotion of Oregon's legacy of authors, poets, and literature?

A. Walt Curtis.

Q. What happened to the cabbages in Walt Curtis's poem "The Cabbages in My Garden"?

A. They were given to an orphanage because he couldn't stand to see them become either cole slaw or sauerkraut.

Q. Who wrote *Mara, Daughter of the Nile* and *Pharaoh*?

A. Eloise McGraw.

Q. Who posed for a poster that urged people to "Expose yourself to art"?

A. Bud Clark, before he became mayor of Portland.

Q. Oregon State University's first Rhodes Scholarship went to whom?

A. Knute Buehler, in 1987.

Q. What structure is nicknamed the "Deodorant Building"?

A. The 1000 Broadway Building in Portland, built in 1991 with a "roll-on top."

Q. Where in Oregon did author Zane Grey have a cabin?

A. Near Winkle Bar on the Rogue River.

Q. What came around Cape Horn in 1837 and was presented to Anna Maria Pittman on the day she married Jason Lee?

A. Oregon's first cultivated rose.

Q. Who wrote *Stories That Could Be True: New and Collected Poems*?

A. William Stafford (1977).

Q. What book by Robin Cody tells the story of three young people coming of age in a small Oregon logging town?

A. *Ricochet River.*

Q. What Portland-born radical poet and communist activist wrote *Ten Days That Shook the World,* basis of the 1980 film *Reds*?

A. John Silas Reed.

Q. What restored French Renaissance mansion furnished with European and American antiques commands a panoramic view of Portland and the Cascades?

A. Pittock Mansion (built around 1914 by Henry Pittock, the publisher who established the *Oregonian* as the state's major newspaper).

Q. What Oregon author, journalist, and historian wrote about the Northwest in *Far Corner* and about old-time logging in *Holy Old Mackinaw*?

A. Stewart Holbrook.

Q. When was the term "webfoot" first applied to Oregonians?

A. During the California gold rush, as a pejorative to those who came early, got their gold, and went back to their soggy homelands.

Q. What is known as "Oregon mist"?

A. Long, steady rain.

———∞———

Q. Where may these words of C. E. S. Wood be seen today: "Good Citizens Are the Riches of a City"?

A. Engraved on the Skidmore Fountain in Portland.

———∞———

Q. In the 1920s who introduced mythic logger Paul Bunyan to a wide audience?

A. James Stevens (1891–1972).

———∞———

Q. Who wrote *The Winds of Morning, Beulah Land, The Distant Music,* and *The Kettle of Fire*?

A. H. L. Davis.

———∞———

Q. What is an "Oregon block and tackle"?

A. Loggers belaying a line on a stump instead of a pulley.

———∞———

Q. Where did the seven-story, chateau-style Portland Hotel stand before it was razed in 1950?

A. On the site of present-day Pioneer Courthouse Square.

———∞———

Q. In what year did the Oregon Pops begin?

A. 1970.

Q. What inspired the builders of the 125-foot-tall Astoria Column?

A. Trajan's Column in Rome.

Q. Who is the founder and current conductor of the Oregon Pops?

A. Norman Leyden.

Q. What is an "Oregon puddin' foot"?

A. A horse bred from a draft horse and a riding horse for mountain farming (also called an Oregon bigfoot).

Q. The statue *Sacajawea* by Alice Cooper was dedicated in Portland's Washington Park by whom?

A. Susan B. Anthony, in 1904 at the opening of the Lewis and Clark Centennial Exposition.

Q. What is the present name of Pacific Academy, founded in 1870?

A. George Fox University, in Newberg.

Q. Author Sam Simpson received what type of degree from Willamette University?

A. Law.

Q. What two presidents are commemorated in the South Park Blocks?

A. Abraham Lincoln and Theodore Roosevelt.

Q. Who said: "You can't learn to write a book by riding a horse any more than you can learn to ride a horse by reading a book"?

A. Reuban A. Long, the "Sage of the Sagebrush" (1898–1974).

─────❈❈❈─────

Q. What author is reputed to have written portions of *End of the Story* at the Wolf Creek Tavern north of Grants Pass?

A. Jack London.

─────❈❈❈─────

Q. Who was Oregon's first poet laureate, author of "The Gold-Gated West" and "Beautiful Willamette"?

A. Sam Simpson.

─────❈❈❈─────

Q. Who sculpted *The Elk,* which stands beside the Multnomah County Courthouse?

A. Roland Perry.

─────❈❈❈─────

Q. How does the refrain to Sam Simpson's "Beautiful Willamette" begin?

A. *Onward ever, lovely river / Softly calling to the sea.*

─────❈❈❈─────

Q. In Chinook Jargon, a hybrid of the Native American language and English, what is the word for "heart"?

A. *Tum-tum.*

Q. Why did Masui Yasui, a Japanese immigrant-turned-businessman and orchardist, decide to stay in Hood River in 1903?

A. Because Mount Hood reminded him of Mount Fuji, causing him to abandon plans to proceed to Cincinnati.

Q. What Portland lawyer founded both the city's library and art museum in addition to writing many progressive laws?

A. C. E. S. Wood (1852–1944).

Q. The *Bridge of the Gods* by what author is still in print after 100 years?

A. Fredric Homer Balch (1861–1891).

Q. Walt Morey, author of Gentle Ben and other stories for children, lived where?

A. Near Wilsonville, in a beautiful hazelnut orchard on the banks of the Willamette River.

Q. Whose short story collections are titled *Highway Trade* and *Bedlam*?

A. John Dominic, professor of English at Linfield College in McMinville.

Q. The literary magazines, *Denali, Silverfish, Northwest Review, Two Girls Review,* and *Fireweed: Poetry of Western Oregon* are all published in what city?

A. Eugene.

Q. M. K. Wren is the pen name of what Oregon author?

A. Martha Kay Renfroe.

Q. What Beaverton author's entries in Bantam Books' *Star Wars* series include *Time Was, Nightmare Asylum, Earth Hive,* and *Shadows of the Empire*?

A. Steve Perry.

Q. What Oregonian's fictional book *Arabian Jazz* received critical acclaim?

A. Diana Abu-Jaber.

Q. What editor of *The Oregonian* served as a Pulitzer Prize juror six times?

A. William A. Hilliard.

Q. Who conducted photographic workshops at the Museum School in Portland from 1959 to 1967, influencing many of Oregon's fine-art photographers?

A. Minor White.

Q. Native American mythology figures prominently in the works of what Newport artist known for his use of pastels and graphite?

A. Rick Bartow.

Q. What Oregonian wrote *Geek Love*, published in 1989?

A. Katherine Dunn.

Q. To what experience does Portland artist Michael Brophy attribute the "hard look" of his paintings?

A. His one-year residency at Studio Arts Center International in Florence, Italy.

———⊗⊗⊗———

Q. What is a recurring subject of Portlander Gregory Grenon's paintings?

A. Women's faces.

———⊗⊗⊗———

Q. Who designed nearly every important building in Eugene from 1886 to 1905?

A. Lord Nelson (Nels) Roney, whose Villard Hall (University of Oregon) and other structures still stand.

———⊗⊗⊗———

Q. In 1962 James DePriest, music director of the Oregon Symphony since 1980, discovered his true calling when he was invited to conduct what orchestra?

A. Bangkok Symphony.

———⊗⊗⊗———

Q. Who authored *A Gift Upon the Shore* and *Curiosity Didn't Kill The Cat*?

A. M. K. Wren.

———⊗⊗⊗———

Q. Who won the Oregon Book Award for the novel *Fight Club*, which a reviewer called "an anthem to our generation who worships at the altar of nihilism and violence"?

A. Chuck Palahnuik.

Q. Who inspired Ursula K. LeGuin to create Harriet, a character in *Catwings*?

A. Lorenzo, her late cat.

———

Q. The University of Oregon's Deady Hall, completed in 1876 and now listed on the National Register of Historic Places, is an example of what style of architecture?

A. Second Empire.

———

Q. For what are Toni Pimble, Julian Stites, and Elena Carter best known?

A. Dance and choreography.

———

Q. What longtime staffer at Portland's Washington Park Zoo has written many children's books featuring animals?

A. Roland Smith.

———

Q. What benefits did poet Lawson Fusao Inada find in Ashland?

A. "California without the madness, the Northwest without the rain."

———

Q. For what books is Jean Auel best known?

A. *The Clan of the Cave Bear, The Mammoth Hunters, Valley of Horses, Plains of Passage.*

———

Q. What is the Fishtrap Gathering?

A. A conference for northwestern writers, journalists, and others in publishing, held each July near Wallowa Lake.

Q. Who garnered a Mary Jane Carr Young Readers Award from Oregon Book Awards for *Under the Blood-Red Sun* and *Blue Skin of the Sea*?

A. Graham Salisbury.

—∞∞—

Q. Kristy Edmunds, contemporary arts curator at the Portland Art Museum from 1990 to 1997, credits what event as the inspiration for *Partito,* an interdisciplinary production featuring a hospital bed?

A. Her great-grandmother's final days in a nursing home.

—∞∞—

Q. What view of history did Washington Irving take in his successful novel *Astoria*?

A. History as romance and adventure.

—∞∞—

Q. How many books were checked out of the Multnomah County Library in fiscal year 1997?

A. Approximately 8.3 million.

—∞∞—

Q. Who brought John Updike, Garrison Keillor, Maya Angelou, and Henry Louis Gates Jr. to Portland's Arlene Schnitzer Concert Hall not once but twice?

A. Portland Arts & Lectures.

—∞∞—

Q. What author's *Cat Scratch Fever* was nominated for an Oregon Book Award?

A. Tara K. Harper.

SPORTS & LEISURE

C H A P T E R   F I V E

Q. What golfing event is sometimes called "Peter's Party"?

A. Fred Meyer Golf Tournament, promoted by Portland-area resident Peter Jacobsen.

Q. Who operated the first ski shop on Mount Hood?

A. Hjalmar Hvam, who coached the 1952 U.S. Nordic combined Olympic team.

Q. What NFL Hall of Famer played for Portland's Jefferson High School, the University of Oregon, and the Dallas Cowboys?

A. Mel Renfro.

Q. What distance runner operates a popular sports training facility near Mount Hood?

A. Alberto Salazar.

Q. What was Oregon's first professional football team?

A. Portland Breakers, who played in the USFL in 1985.

Q. Victorian Days and the World Timber Carnival are held each July in what city?

A. Albany.

———— ∞∞∞ ————

Q. What former Portland State University quarterback was enshrined in the College Football Hall of Fame in 1996?

A. Neil Lomax.

———— ∞∞∞ ————

Q. What is the largest rainbow trout ever pulled from Oregon waters?

A. 28 lbs., 0 oz., by Mike McGonagle in 1982 from the Rogue River.

———— ∞∞∞ ————

Q. In what league do the Portland Winter Hawks play?

A. Western Hockey League.

———— ∞∞∞ ————

Q. The University of Oregon played what team in the 1995 Cotton Bowl?

A. University of Colorado.

———— ∞∞∞ ————

Q. In what year did the Rose Quarter complex open in Portland?

A. 1995.

———— ∞∞∞ ————

Q. What is the seating capacity of the Rose Garden for Portland Trail Blazers home games?

A. 21,400.

Q. A statue of what animal graces the city park in Winston?

A. Cheetah (in recognition of the breeding program at nearby Wildlife Safari).

Q. What impact does the annual Round-Up have on the population of Pendleton?

A. It causes the city's normal population of 15,000 to double.

Q. What annual event features a quilt show, duck derby, sock hop, car shows, and the Prefontaine Memorial Run?

A. Bay Area Fun Festival, held in September in Coos Bay.

Q. In addition to football, Mel Renfro garnered All-America honors in what sport while attending the University of Oregon?

A. Track (high hurdles and long jump).

Q. How many teams played in the Western Hockey League in 1998?

A. Eighteen.

Q. What was unusual about the University of Portland's 1995 soccer season?

A. The men's and women's teams, both coached by Clive Charles, reached the NCAA Final Four, only the second time in NCAA history that has occurred.

Q. Where was the first Fred Meyer Golf Tournament played?

A. Portland Golf Club, August 17–19, 1986.

Q. What former St. Louis Cardinals quarterback (1981–1988) lived in Lake Oswego as a youth?

A. Neil Lomax.

———

Q. What Oregon locale is considered a wind-surfing mecca?

A. Columbia Gorge from Hood River to Arlington.

———

Q. How many times have the Oregon Ducks faced teams from Pennsylvania in the Rose Bowl?

A. Twice: 1917 (Pennsylvania) and 1995 (Penn State).

———

Q. The 10,000-meter Prefontaine Memorial Run, named in honor of popular Oregon distance runner and Olympian Steve Prefontaine, was established in what year?

A. 1979.

———

Q. Who won the 1942 Rose Bowl game between Oregon State University and Duke?

A. Oregon State, 20–16.

———

Q. After breaking his leg three times, who invented the safety binding for skis?

A. Hjalmar Hvam.

———

Q. In how many Super Bowls did former Duck Mel Renfro play?

A. Three.

Q. What is the largest chinook salmon ever caught in Oregon waters?

A. Approximately 83 lbs., by Earnie St. Clair in 1910 on the Umpqua River.

Q. The Portland Beavers won the Pacific Coast League baseball championship in what years?

A. 1906 and 1945, according to the Oregon Sports Hall of Fame.

Q. How many 20-year-olds may play on a Western Hockey League team?

A. Three.

Q. Through the 1996–97 season, how many times have the Portland Trail Blazers won the NBA Western Conference championship?

A. Three: 1977, 1990, and 1992.

Q. Who quarterbacked Oregon to a 14–0 win over the University of Pennsylvania in the 1917 Rose Bowl?

A. "Shy" Huntington.

Q. From 1977 to 1997, how many times did the Trail Blazers make the NBA playoffs?

A. Eighteen (including 14 consecutive appearances, a league record).

Q. What was Dale Thomas's career coaching record when he retired in 1990 after 33 years as Oregon State University's wrestling coach?

A. 616 wins, 169 losses, and 12 draws.

———— ❧ ————

Q. When do the most people visit the Ochoco National Forest?

A. Late summer and fall (hunting season for mule deer and elk).

———— ❧ ————

Q. Who won the 1958 Rose Bowl game between the University of Oregon and Ohio State?

A. Ohio State, 10–7.

———— ❧ ————

Q. What Portland Trail Blazer played on the U.S. Olympic Dream Team in 1992?

A. Clyde Drexler.

———— ❧ ————

Q. What team beat the Trail Blazers to claim the 1990 NBA championship?

A. Detroit Pistons.

———— ❧ ————

Q. What was the largest crowd ever in attendance at a basketball game in Memorial Coliseum?

A. 12,888.

———— ❧ ————

Q. What was unique about the November 1, 1974, game in Portland's Memorial Coliseum? The Blazers played the Buffalo Braves (now the Los Angeles Clippers) and won 113–106.

A. Gerald Ford was the first U.S. president in history to attend an NBA game as president.

Q. After training at Portland's Multnomah Athletic Club, swimmer Don Schollander won four gold medals at which Olympics?

A. 1964 Summer Games in Tokyo.

Q. What OSU All-American played on the 1964 U.S. Olympic basketball team?

A. Mel Kouzan.

Q. According to *Golf Digest*, which nine-hole course plays longer, Lakeridge Golf & Country Club in Lakeview or Valley Golf Course in Hines?

A. Lakeridge (3,346 yards) is slightly longer than Valley (3,215 yards).

Q. What Oregon team became the women's world softball champions in 1944?

A. Erv Lind Florists, Portland.

Q. What Ames native placed second in the Indianapolis 500 in 1962?

A. Len Sutton.

Q. In what year did the University of Oregon track and field team win its first NCAA championship?

A. 1962.

Q. In what year did the Ladies Professional Golf Association stage its first tournament in Oregon?

A. 1972, at Portland's Columbia Edgewater Golf Course.

Q. In what event did Oregonian Bill Dillinger win a bronze medal in the 1964 Olympics?

A. 5,000-meter run.

Q. As of January 1998, how many Heisman Trophy winners have come from Oregon colleges?

A. One: Terry Baker of Oregon State University (1962).

Q. What feat did tennis player Jack Neer accomplish in 1961?

A. He won his seventh consecutive Oregon Open men's championship.

Q. After being tabbed in the preseason to finish last, who won the Western Hockey League championship for the 1960–61 season?

A. Portland Buckeroos.

Q. From 1961 until 1979, what fitness personality's show that originated from Portland's KGW-TV was carried via repeater links throughout Oregon?

A. Joe Loprinzi.

Q. Who defeated the Portland Trail Blazers to win the NBA championship in 1992?

A. Chicago Bulls.

Q. What 14-year-old Oregon swimmer was a member of the gold medal-winning relay team at the Rome Olympics in 1960?

A. Carolyn Wood.

Q. When did the Portland Memorial Coliseum open?

A. 1960.

Q. What nickname was given to the 20 businessmen who organized the first professional golf tournament in the state?

A. "Trembling Twenty," because of their inexperience in golf promotion.

Q. How many games did the OSU Beavers win during the 1955 football season?

A. One.

Q. Who was the first Oregon Duck to run the mile in under four minutes?

A. Jim Bailey, who broke the tape at 3:58.6 in 1956 at the Los Angeles Coliseum.

Q. In what sport did Oregonian Jean Soubert win two medals at the 1964 Winter Olympics in Innsbruck?

A. Downhill skiing.

Q. What University of Oregon quarterback signed with the Baltimore Colts as the No. 1 draft pick in 1954?

A. George Shaw.

Q. In what years did amateur golfer Grace DeMoss Zwahlen of Corvallis represent the United States in Curtis Cup competition against the British?

A. 1952 and 1954.

Q. Prior to the opening of Parker Stadium in 1953, what venue was home to the OSU football team?

A. Bell Field.

Q. A 1952 preseason football game at Multnomah Stadium featured what two teams that have since moved to other cities?

A. Los Angeles Rams (moved to St. Louis) and Chicago Cardinals (moved to St. Louis, then to Phoenix).

Q. Who founded the Portland Trail Blazers franchise?

A. Harry Glickman.

Q. When did the Blazers begin playing in Portland?

A. 1970.

Q. Who quarterbacked the University of Oregon to an appearance in the 1948 Cotton Bowl game?

A. Norm Van Brocklin.

Q. Who was Jack Cody?

A. Renowned swimming coach (1914–1949) at the Multnomah Athletic Club whose "Cody Kids" of the 1940s won a host of individual, team, and national championships as well as Olympic gold in the women's 4 x 100 freestyle relay at the 1948 Games in London.

Q. What businessman brought the British golf team to Portland in 1947 at his own expense, keeping the Ryder Cup alive?

A. Bob Hudson.

Q. Oregon State played against what team in the 1957 Rose Bowl?

A. Iowa.

Q. In what year did Tom Prothro begin coaching OSU football?

A. 1956.

Q. How old was Oregon-born Joe Nutxhall when he pitched for the Cincinnati Reds in 1944?

A. Fifteen.

Q. Who pitched the Erv Lind Florists to the 1944 women's world softball championship?

A. Betty Evans, at age 18.

Q. In what year did Salem native A. C. Gilbert clear 12 feet, 2 inches to win Olympic gold in the pole vault?

A. 1908, in London.

Q. For whom is Gill Coliseum at Oregon State University named?

A. Basketball coach "Slats" Gill.

Q. What octet of link stars played in the first Fred Meyer Golf Tournament held in Portland?

A. Peter Jacobsen, Fred Couples, Curtis Strange, Fuzzy Zoeller, Greg Norman, Gary Player, Arnold Palmer, and Tom Watson.

Q. When did Les Steers of the University of Oregon set a world record in the high jump at 6 feet, 11 inches?

A. 1941, at the Pacific Coast-Big Ten meet at UCLA.

Q. What organization introduced football to Oregon in 1890?

A. Multnomah Athletic Club, which fielded the first team in the state.

Q. In the 1930s and '40s, what groundskeeper befriended countless young Portland Beaver fans at the Vaughn Street Baseball Park?

A. Rocky Benevento.

Q. To what does the nickname "Tall Firs" refer?

A. The University of Oregon basketball team that in 1939 became the first West Coast squad to win the NCAA championship.

Q. What medal did Mack Robinson of Portland win at the 1936 Olympics in Berlin?

A. Silver, in the 200-meter run.

———————

Q. Who is Oregon's winningest high school football coach?

A. Don Requa, who coached at Pendleton High from the 1950s into the '80s and compiled a 273-86-5 record over his 36-year career.

———————

Q. In what event did George Baroff of the University of Oregon set a world record in 1936?

A. Pole vault (14 feet, 6.5 inches).

———————

Q. What feat earned the 1933 Oregon State football team the nickname "Iron Men"?

A. Using only 11 players (no substitutes), OSU held powerful USC to a 0–0 tie at Multnomah Stadium.

———————

Q. In what event did Ralph Hill of Klamath County earn a silver medal at the 1932 Los Angeles Olympics?

A. 5,000-meter run.

———————

Q. What prep All-American led the McMinnville High School Grizzlies to the state basketball tournament three times and the AAA title in 1979?

A. Charlie Sitton.

Q. In what year was the last football game played between the Multnomah Athletic Club and the University of Oregon?

A. 1925.

Q. What player had the longest tenure with the Portland Beavers?

A. Eddie Basinski, who played 14 seasons (1947–1960) for the baseball team.

Q. What discus thrower brought home the gold in the 1976 Montreal Olympics?

A. Mack Wilkins of Eugene.

Q. What was the first season the OSU Beavers played basketball in Gill Coliseum?

A. 1949–50.

Q. Where did 1924 Olympic medalists Robin Reed and Lester Newton both train?

A. Multnomah Athletic Club.

Q. In what year did the University of Oregon play Harvard in the Rose Bowl?

A. 1920 (Oregon won 7–6).

Q. What two-time basketball All-American helped OSU post a 93–25 record during his four years as a starter before signing with the Dallas Mavericks?

A. Charlie Sitton.

———— ∞∞∞ ————

Q. Where in Oregon may one find a scenic auto route that offers rugged towers, deep gorges, and bright splashes of color on sandstone cliffs at twilight and dawn?

A. Leslie Gulch-Succor Creek National Back Country Byway, near Ontario.

———— ∞∞∞ ————

Q. Where was the first basketball tournament played in Oregon?

A. Salem, in 1920.

———— ∞∞∞ ————

Q. The Portland Beavers advanced to the Pacific Coast League pennant game five consecutive times in what years?

A. 1910–1914, but they lost all five championship games.

———— ∞∞∞ ————

Q. When was the Multnomah Athletic Club founded?

A. 1891.

———— ∞∞∞ ————

Q. When was Bill Hayward track and field coach at the University of Oregon?

A. 1904–1947 (the stadium there was named for him).

Q. Tom DeSilvia of the Philadelphia Eagles attended what three Oregon high schools?

A. Jefferson, Grant, and David Douglas, all in Portland.

Q. What Woodburn resident played for the New York Giants, then coached the Pittsburgh Steelers, among other teams?

A. Bill Austin.

Q. What Oregon athlete has been enshrined in the World Softball Hall of Fame?

A. Margaret Dobson.

Q. Who said of Portland's Vaughn Street Baseball Park, "The fans could get so close to the players and talk to them"?

A. Eddie Basinski.

Q. Who coached Eastern Oregon University to three straight conference basketball championships?

A. E. Robert Quinn of La Grande.

Q. What basketball All-American led the 1963 OSU Beavers to the NCAA Final Four?

A. Jim Jarvis of Roseburg.

Q. Where did distance runner Steve Prefontaine begin his career?

A. Marshfield High in Coos Bay.

———⚬∞⚬———

Q. Who set a world record of 11.1 seconds in the 100-meter sprint at the 1968 Olympic trials?

A. Margaret Johnson Bailes, a student at Eugene High School.

———⚬∞⚬———

Q. In 10 years with the San Diego Padres, Corvallis native Dave Roberts played every position except what?

A. Pitcher.

———⚬∞⚬———

Q. What Oregon native was a member of the first U.S. tennis team to visit China, in 1983?

A. Emory Neale of Portland.

———⚬∞⚬———

Q. What coach guided Medford High School teams to four state football championships and 23 Southern Oregon Conference titles?

A. Fred Speigelberg, who coached at Medford High from 1948 to 1983.

———⚬∞⚬———

Q. Where was basketball Olympian Carol Menken-Schaudt born?

A. Jefferson.

Q. When did the Multnomah Athletic Club last play football against Oregon State University?

A. 1926.

Q. What was football coach Bill McArthur's career win-loss record at Western Oregon?

A. 185–115–7.

Q. What Woodland-born pro boxer was known as the "Fighting Farmer"?

A. Joseph John Kahut.

Q. When did dragon boat racing become a part of the Portland Rose Festival?

A. 1988.

Q. What player saw his No. 45 jersey retired by the Portland Trail Blazers?

A. Geoff Petrie.

Q. Coach Ralph Miller guided the OSU Beavers to how many Pacific-10 basketball titles?

A. Four: 1980, 1981, 1982, and 1984.

Q. Who was the first man from Oregon to win an Olympic medal?

A. Bert H. W. Kerrigan, in the broad jump in 1906.

Q. What Oregonian was the top-ranked U.S. senior tennis player in 1966 and 1969?

A. Emory Neale.

Q. How many medalists in the 1984 Olympics hailed from Oregon?

A. Eight.

Q. Who did *Sports Illustrated* name the 1989 consensus All-America College Basketball Player of the Year?

A. Gary Payton of Oregon State University.

Q. How many Oregonians won Olympic gold medals at the 1996 Summer Games in Atlanta?

A. Five: Dan O'Brien (decathlon), Gary Payton (basketball), and Shannon McMillan, Tiffany Milbert, and Katy Steding (basketball).

Q. Who won the New York City Marathon three times, the Boston Marathon twice, and was a member of the 1980 and 1984 U.S. Olympic teams?

A. Alberto Salazar.

Q. In what year was the Portland Beavers Baseball Club organized?

A. 1905.

Q. Which Oregon River has a style of drift boat named after it?

A. McKenzie.

Q. What Oregon records did runner Steve Prefontaine hold?

A. Every record from two miles to six miles and the metric equivalents.

———∞∞∞———

Q. What team did the Trail Blazers beat to win the NBA championship in 1977?

A. Philadelphia 76ers.

———∞∞∞———

Q. What Oregon native became the first American woman to clear more than six feet in the high jump?

A. Joni Huntley (the feat earned her a gold medal at the 1975 Pan-American Games).

———∞∞∞———

Q. Fishermen consider what town the dividing line between the upper and lower Deschutes River?

A. Maupin.

———∞∞∞———

Q. In 1989, when Ralph Miller coached his last basketball game for Oregon State, how did fans show their respect for his 20-year (1970–1989) career at the school?

A. They wore tuxedos to the game, played at Corvallis against archrival Oregon.

———∞∞∞———

Q. By 1986 Ad Rutschman had Coached the Linfield College football team to how many NAIA championships?

A. Three.

Q. How did Portland State University honor Lynda Johnson when she became the first four-time All-America volleyball player in NCAA Division II history?

A. Her number was retired.

———∞———

Q. Who captured the gold medal in downhill skiing at the 1982 Sarajevo Olympics?

A. Bill Johnson of Sandy.

———∞———

Q. What Oregon native won three Olympic gold medals for swimming in 1920?

A. Norman Ross.

———∞———

Q. Who was the state weightlifting champion of 1936?

A. Joe Loprinzi, television fitness personality and longtime athletic director at the Multnomah Athletic Club.

———∞———

Q. What was remarkable about the Oregon Ducks' 1981 football season?

A. They won their first nine games and were ranked No. 1 in the Pacific-10 Conference for nine weeks.

———∞———

Q. What was the average salary of a Portland Trail Blazer in 1996?

A. $1.67 million.

Q. The average annual salary of a Portland Beaver baseball player in the 1950s was how much?

A. Approximately $7,000.

Q. In 1978 Portland hosted what championship sporting event?

A. U.S. figure skating championships.

Q. What basketball player holds the career scoring record at Portland State?

A. Freeman Williams, with 3,249 points (second in the NCAA to Pete Maravich of LSU).

Q. For how many seasons had Jack Ramsey coached the Trail Blazers when they won the NBA championship in 1977?

A. One.

Q. Who was voted Oregon's top amateur athlete in 1976?

A. Track and field star Mack Wilkins.

Q. Who was the prime mover in forming the Portland Beavers baseball franchise?

A. Walter McCready.

Q. Who in 1973 became the first athlete to win four successive NCAA championships in the same event?

A. Steve Prefontaine of the University of Oregon, in the 5,000-meter run.

Q. How many times was Oregon's Larry Mahan named all-round national rodeo champion?

A. Six.

Q. Who was named the NBA's Most Valuable Player in 1977?

A. Bill Walton, center for the Portland Trail Blazers.

Q. University of Oregon's Ahmad Rashad played in how many NFL Pro Bowls?

A. Four.

Q. What Dayton-born athlete, just out of high school, won the U.S. women's amateur golf title in 1972?

A. Mary Budke.

Q. Who was the first American to win the world freestyle wrestling championship?

A. Rick Sanders of Portland State University, in 1969.

Q. What was baseball player Eddie Basinski's musical avocation?

A. Concert violinist.

Q. What team formed by several Madison High School baseball players won the American Legion World Series in 1969?

A. Contractors, Inc.

Q. Who won the men's and women's titles at the 1978 U.S. figure skating championship?

A. Charles Tickner and Linda Fratianne.

———⊗———

Q. What former Lincoln High School state champion pitched for the world champion 1968 Detroit Tigers?

A. Mickey Lolich.

———⊗———

Q. In how many rodeos did Larry Mahan ride?

A. More than 1,200.

———⊗———

Q. What guard joined the Trail Blazers during the 1976–77 season after a four-year stint in the American Basketball Association?

A. Dave Twardzik.

———⊗———

Q. Olympic gold medalist Dick Fosbury developed the "Fosbury Flop," his unique approach to the high jump, while attending what secondary school?

A. Medford High School.

———⊗———

Q. Who authored the book *Jogging*?

A. Bill Bowerman, co-founder of Nike.

———⊗———

Q. What was the average annual salary of a Portland Buckeroo hockey player during the 1960s?

A. About $5,000.

Q. What former Trail Blazer in 1996 was voted as one of the NBA's 50 greatest players in the league's first 50 years?

A. Bill Walton.

—————

Q. Who were the "Giant Killers"?

A. The 1967 Oregon State football team, which defeated top-ranked Purdue as well as UCLA and USC during a four-week span.

—————

Q. Who won the 1967 U.S. Women's Open bowling championship?

A. Gloria Bouvia of Gresham.

—————

Q. Who may participate in the Pacific Amateur Golf Classic held annually on five Central Oregon courses?

A. Amateur golfers of all abilities who possess an established USGA Slope Handicap.

—————

Q. What was the only bowl game in which Terry Baker played for OSU?

A. 1962 Liberty Bowl.

—————

Q. What accolade did *Golf Digest* confer on the Crosswater Golf Course at Sunriver in 1995?

A. Best New Resort Course.

—————

Q. Skiers and their dogs compete in what cross-country race held the second weekend in February at the Hoodoo Bowl on Oregon 126 east of Springfield?

A. Skijoring.

Q. Where is the Pole, Paddle, Pedal race held each September?

A. The ski, canoe, and bicycle race starts at Mount Bachelor and ends in Bend's Drake Park.

Q. In addition to selling fly-fishing gear and crafts, what shop in Bend on the banks of the Deschutes River offers casting classes for new anglers?

A. Numb-Butt Fly Company.

Q. Before coming to Portland, the Breakers pro football team played for what other cities?

A. Boston (1983) and New Orleans (1984).

Q. During his 16-year career in professional baseball, how many shutouts did Mickey Lolich pitch?

A. Forty-one.

Q. How many minor league baseball teams called Portland home in 1994?

A. None; the Beavers had moved to Salt Lake City and the Rockies had yet to arrive from Bend.

Q. Besides dangers inherent to their sport, what else must wind-surfers on the Columbia River be wary of?

A. Barge traffic.

Q. Who promoted the 1952 preseason football game at Multnomah Stadium between the Los Angeles Rams and Chicago Cardinals?

A. Harry Glickman.

Q. When Mack Robinson won the silver medal in the 200-meter run at the 1936 Berlin Olympics, who captured the gold?

A. Jesse Owens.

Q. Who coached the University of Oregon to a 7–6 win over Harvard in the 1920 Rose Bowl game?

A. "Shy" Huntington.

Q. What Oregonian was the first American tennis player to win the men's singles championship at Wimbledon?

A. Bill Tilden, in 1929.

Q. Who dedicated the original clubhouse at the Multnomah Athletic Club?

A. Theodore Roosevelt.

Q. In what year was Oregon gridiron great Bill Austin named All-Pro by UPI?

A. 1955.

Q. What was Portland Beaver second baseman Eddie Basinski's career batting average?

A. .261.

Q. The current national high school record of 8 minutes, 41 seconds for the two-mile run was set by whom?

A. Steve Prefontaine, in 1968.

Q. Who was professional baseball's No. 1 draft pick in 1972?

A. Dave Roberts of the University of Oregon (selected by the San Diego Padres).

Q. What was Joseph John Kahut's professional career boxing record?

A. 56 wins, 24 losses, 7 draws.

Q. After retiring as a player, Geoff Petrie served in what other capacities with the Portland Trail Blazers?

A. Broadcaster, shooting coach, and executive.

Q. When Oregonian Joannie Huntley posted a personal best of 6 feet, 5.5 inches in the high jump at the 1984 Los Angeles Olympics, how old was she?

A. Twenty-eight.

Q. How many Western Hockey League championships have the Portland Winter Hawks won?

A. Two: 1987 and 1998.

Q. Who was the hero for Oregon State in the 1962 Liberty Bowl?

A. Terry Baker, whose 99-yard run led the Beavers to a 6–0 victory over Villanova.

Q. Who trained at the University of Oregon, represented Brazil, and earned a gold medal in the 800 meters at the 1984 Summer Games in Los Angeles?

A. Joaquim Cruz.

———∞∞∞———

Q. In how many NFL Pro Bowls did former Portland State grid star Neil Lomax appear?

A. Two: 1984 and 1987.

———∞∞∞———

Q. How many games did the Trail Blazers lose in the 1977 NBA Championship Series before winning four straight from the Philadelphia 76ers to capture the title?

A. Two.

———∞∞∞———

Q. What former University of Oregon star led the NFL in receptions in 1977 and 1979?

A. Ahmad Rashad.

———∞∞∞———

Q. By his own estimation, how many bucking broncos and bulls did rodeo champ Larry Mahan ride during his professional career?

A. Approximately 6,000.

———∞∞∞———

Q. On how many NBA championship teams did Bill Walton play?

A. Two: Portland Trail Blazers (1976–77) and Boston Celtics (1985–86).

———∞∞∞———

Q. What do wind-surfers in the Columbia Gorge do to fight hypothermia?

A. Wear wetsuits.

SCIENCE & NATURE

Q. Who developed the maraschino cherry?

A. Researchers at Oregon State University.

———✦———

Q. Why do the branches of trees in the Columbia Gorge all grow pointing in one direction?

A. Because of steady prevailing winds that blow through the gorge.

———✦———

Q. What are anadromous fish?

A. Fish that migrate from the ocean to fresh water to spawn, such as salmon.

———✦———

Q. The world's tallest cedar tree, soaring 219 feet, may be seen where?

A. Port Orford.

———✦———

Q. How many species of Oregon marine and coastal life can be found at the Oregon Coast Aquarium in Newport?

A. About 200.

Q. When the Willamette River flooded Portland in 1894, how many city blocks were underwater?

A. 250.

———⊗⊗⊗———

Q. How hot are the Bagby Hot Springs?

A. 136 degrees Fahrenheit.

———⊗⊗⊗———

Q. When Intel opened an Oregon plant in 1974, what three locally based technology firms were already well established?

A. Tektronix, Electro Scientific Industries, and Floating Point Systems.

———⊗⊗⊗———

Q. What museum boasts a desertarium featuring small regional animals in a natural environment?

A. Oregon High Desert Museum in Bend.

———⊗⊗⊗———

Q. Swainson's hawk, which summers in Oregon, migrates to what country for the winter?

A. Argentina.

———⊗⊗⊗———

Q. Oregon State University conducts ocean research aboard what vessel?

A. *Wecoma.*

———⊗⊗⊗———

Q. What was Tektronix's first product?

A. Series 511 oscilloscope (made primarily from World War II government surplus).

Q. How did the eruption of Mount Saint Helens affect the channel of the Columbia River?

A. Ash and mud reduced its normal 40-foot depth to just 14 feet.

———⚬∞⚬———

Q. What distinguishes Mount Thielson in southern Oregon from other volcanic mountains?

A. Its exposed central plug has created a spire-like peak.

———⚬∞⚬———

Q. Of the Three Sisters mountains, which one is the oldest?

A. North Sister (at 10,085 feet, it's also the tallest and toughest to climb).

———⚬∞⚬———

Q. How does the western rattlesnake locate its prey?

A. Sensory organs that can detect heat.

———⚬∞⚬———

Q. How did the Douglas fir receive its name?

A. The tree was named by and for David Douglas, a naturalist who toured the Pacific Northwest in the 1820s on behalf of the Royal Horticultural Society.

———⚬∞⚬———

Q. Why do scientists believe the Klamath-Siskiyou Mountains were once at the bottom of the sea?

A. Rocks present in the mountain can only be formed on deep ocean floors under intense pressure.

Q. What was the average depth of volcanic ash 10 miles downwind following the 1981 eruption of Mount Saint Helens?

A. Ten inches.

———❊———

Q. What artifacts may be viewed at the Visitors Center of the John Day National Monument?

A. Fossils recovered from the John Day Basin.

———❊———

Q. How long is the Oregon Coast Trail?

A. 360 miles, from the South Jetty of the Columbia River to the California border.

———❊———

Q. What is the source of the Metolius River?

A. A spring called the "Spring" in Jefferson County.

———❊———

Q. In addition to the Klamath-Siskiyou Mountains, what other Oregon highlands were once on the ocean floor?

A. Hells Canyon (the area contains limestone reefs and fossils of sea life).

———❊———

Q. During the spring what blankets the fields along U.S. 101 south of Brookings?

A. Lilies.

Q. What equipment should a wildlife observer take on a night-time trek through Oregon's high desert country?

A. Snakeproof boots and a flashlight with a red lens to minimize pupil dilation if light is needed for a closer look at the terrain or wildlife.

Q. What is the significance of the large chimney in George Rogers Memorial Park in Lake Oswego?

A. It was once attached to the smelter of Oswego Iron Works, focal point of the "Pittsburgh of the West."

Q. What is the origin of the bighorn sheep that inhabit Steens Mountain and Hart Mountain National Antelope Refuge?

A. Wildlife rangers reintroduced the present herd from other areas after the native stock had been overhunted or killed by a domestic sheep disease.

Q. What exposed monolith is second in size only to the Rock of Gibraltar?

A. Beacon Rock, which is visible from Bonneville Dam and all along the Columbia Gorge.

Q. What is the Yolla Bolly Terrane?

A. Tectonic plate that runs along the southern Oregon coast.

Q. How many species of butterflies can be found in Oregon?

A. About 225.

Q. What percentage of Oregon's power supply is generated from hydroelectric dams?

A. Approximately 60 percent.

———— ∞ ————

Q. What is an Oregon oredon?

A. Ancestor of the pig that roamed the John Day region during the Oligocene era.

———— ∞ ————

Q. How many Swainson's hawks are there?

A. An estimated 400,000 to 500,000.

———— ∞ ————

Q. What company makes most of the machine-readable laser optical scanners used by supermarkets and retailers worldwide?

A. Spectra-Physics Scanning Systems in Eugene.

———— ∞ ————

Q. When did Mount Hood last erupt?

A. Shortly before Lewis and Clark arrived in Oregon in 1804.

———— ∞ ————

Q. When are the best times to see the gray whale migration off the Oregon coast?

A. Mid-December to mid-January and mid-March to mid-April.

———— ∞ ————

Q. What Calapooyan vision-quest site can now be reached via a paved road?

A. Mary's Peak near Corvallis (tallest point in the Coast Mountains).

Q. Indigenous to the Columbia River, what is America's largest freshwater fish?

A. White sturgeon (the state record catch measured nearly 10 feet).

———— ∞ ————

Q. What is the largest privately held business in Oregon?

A. Jeld-Wen, Inc. in Klamath Falls (selling over $1 billion a year in windows, doors, and millwork).

———— ∞ ————

Q. How many miles do gray whales cover on an average day?

A. About 100.

———— ∞ ————

Q. How was the Tektronix Series 511 different from earlier oscilloscopes?

A. It could see the full signal of high-speed events.

———— ∞ ————

Q. What is the northernmost point on the 40-mile loop trail around Portland?

A. Kelley Point Park.

———— ∞ ————

Q. How high does Cascade Head rise above the ocean?

A. 1,600 feet.

———— ∞ ————

Q. What two mesas in the Agate Desert are separated by Sam's Valley?

A. Upper Table Rock and Lower Table Rock.

Q. How many gray whales exist in the wild?

A. Approximately 21,000.

Q. How did the citizens of Roseburg predict rain prior to the interstate highway construction on Mount Emil?

A. Goats coming down from the mountain (human development has since caused the goats to move on).

Q. What was the estimated volume of ash hurled into the air by the 1981 eruption of Mount Saint Helens?

A. If not compressed, 0.26 cubic miles (landslide debris accounted for another 0.67 cubic miles).

Q. How deep was Lake Chewacan, a remnant of the last Ice Age that once covered much of Lake County?

A. 300 feet (Abert and Summer Lakes are remnants of the much larger and deeper body of water).

Q. Why is eastern Oregon arid while the Willamette Valley is not?

A. Prevailing westerly winds bring in moisture from the Pacific Ocean, but the Cascades prevent rain clouds from continuing eastward.

Q. As a species, how old is the sturgeon?

A. An estimated 375 million years.

Q. What Beaverton company established the laser as a machine tool for microelectronics?

A. Electro Scientific Industries.

———∞———

Q. The stone retaining walls on the Columbia Gorge Scenic Highway were inspired by constructions along what European river?

A. Rhine.

———∞———

Q. Chemist Linus Pauling was born in what Oregon city?

A. Condon, February 28, 1901.

———∞———

Q. Oregon's pronghorn, the fastest animal in North America, can run how fast?

A. 40 mph.

———∞———

Q. What University of Oregon graduate in 1956 received a Nobel Prize in physics for co-inventing the transistor?

A. Walter Brattain.

———∞———

Q. In 1996 what was the ratio of doctors to pharmacists in Oregon?

A. More than four to one (10,793 to 2,484).

———∞———

Q. What is the largest reforestation project ever undertaken by a state?

A. Replanting the Tillamook Burn in 1948 after 350,000 acres were destroyed by fire.

Q. Who developed a retina scanner for purposes of high-security identification?

A. Robert B. Hill, founder of Eyedentify, in 1976.

Q. Where is the world's largest sawmill?

A. Klamath Falls (Weyerhaeuser pine lumber factory).

Q. When it was installed in 1950, where was the longest continuous escalator system in the world?

A. Meier and Frank Department Store in Portland.

Q. How far out to sea does the Columbia River dilute ocean water?

A. More than 300 miles.

Q. Before dams stopped the Columbia's drift of silt, how much sediment did the river carry to the sea each year?

A. More than 7.5 tons.

Q. Who developed the Phillips screw in 1933?

A. Henry F. Phillips (Phillips Screw Company, Portland).

Q. Why is Crater Lake so blue?

A. Its depth (1,932 feet) and clarity of water create the appearance.

Q. With white plumage, black feet and beak, and a distinctive two-note call that can be heard a mile away, what is one of the largest birds that can be seen in Oregon?

A. Trumpeter swan, which often summers in Oregon and averages 35 to 40 pounds with a wing span of 7 to 8 feet.

Q. Why did Charles Ladd buy Beacon Rock at the turn of the century?

A. To save it from being quarried.

Q. Why are fishermen not allowed to keep sturgeon over six feet long?

A. To preserve the fishery, as large females may carry up to 100 pounds of eggs.

Q. What once occupied the site of the present-day Vietnam Veteran's Memorial in Portland?

A. Pitch and putt golf course.

Q. What are the terminal points of the gray whale migration?

A. Lagoons in Baja, Mexico, and the north coast of Alaska.

Q. What inspired lumberjack Joseph B. Cox to invent a better chain saw in 1947?

A. Watching timber beetles.

Q. What formed the many capes of the Oregon coast?

A. Lava flows from ancient volcanoes.

———∞∞———

Q. Why does the sandstone Cape Kiwanda not dissolve in pounding surf?

A. A sea stack of basalt in front of the cape absorbs the water's force.

———∞∞———

Q. Oregon State's College of Forestry manages what two research forests near Corvallis?

A. McDonald and Dunn.

———∞∞———

Q. What animal is also known as the wapiti?

A. American elk.

———∞∞———

Q. In 1909 where was the nation's first school of anesthesiology founded?

A. Saint Vincent Hospital in Portland.

———∞∞———

Q. What Eugene-born doctor in 1948 became the first woman to be elected president of a state medical society?

A. Leslie S. Kent.

———∞∞———

Q. Indigenous to parts of Oregon, what is *Crotalus viridus*?

A. Western rattlesnake.

Q. In 1948 where was the ocular microscope developed?

A. Oregon Health Sciences University in Portland.

Q. Halibut are most profuse off what Oregon coastal city?

A. Newport.

Q. How far have halibut been known to swim?

A. More than 2,500 miles (from the Aleutian Islands to Newport).

Q. Where may one see full-size fiberglass replicas of dinosaurs?

A. Thunderbeast Park, 40 miles north of Klamath Falls on U.S. 97.

Q. How large is the Columbia Plateau, which was formed by prehistoric lava flows?

A. Approximately 200,000 square miles, extending from eastern Oregon into Washington and Idaho.

Q. Where may one see Old Perpetual Geyser?

A. Lakeview.

Q. Oregon sturgeon seldom exceed what length?

A. Twelve feet.

Q. When was the Columbia River Gorge designated a National Scenic Area?

A. 1986.

Q. What is an erratic rock?

A. One moved by a glacier from its original place, as at Erratic Rock State Park near McMinnville.

Q. For whom was Depoe Bay named?

A. Willie DePoe, and Indian trader.

Q. Compared to humans, how much more sensitive to light are the eyes of owls?

A. Between 35 times and 100 times.

Q. What did aeronautic engineers learn from owl feathers?

A. How to make jet engines operate more quietly.

Q. How long do steelhead trout remain in the ocean?

A. Two to three years.

Q. How did Hardtack Island, south of Ross Island in the Willamette, receive its name?

A. Originally called Hardhack Island, due to native vegetation, sailors corrupted the name to Hardtack Island for navigational coincidences.

Q. Where was plywood invented?

A. Portland, for the 1904 Lewis and Clark Centennial Exposition.

Q. What three National Wildlife Refuges were established as wintering areas for dusky Canada geese in the Willamette Valley?

A. William Finley, Ankeny, and Baskett Slough.

Q. In 1960 where did Doctors Albert Starr and Miles Lowell Edwards implant the first Starr-Edwards artificial heart valve?

A. Oregon Health Sciences University, Portland.

Q. In 1912 where was the first laboratory built exclusively for pathology?

A. Saint Vincent Hospital in Portland.

Q. What portion of Oregon's highway funds is reserved for the construction of bicycle paths?

A. One percent.

Q. What is the origin of Beacon Rock?

A. It was the core of a volcano, active nine million years ago.

Q. Where in Coos County can one find a large concentration of the rare giant coastal bog lily *(Lilium occidentale)*?

A. Bastendorf Bog.

———— ∞ ————

Q. What type of bears live in Oregon?

A. Black bears.

———— ∞ ————

Q. What percentage of the U.S. hazelnut crop is grown in Oregon?

A. Ninety-nine percent.

———— ∞ ————

Q. Once they spawn, do steelhead trout return to the ocean?

A. Yes, they may repeat the cycle three to five or more times.

———— ∞ ————

Q. In 1844 where did Jessie Applegate operate the first ferry in Oregon?

A. Willamette Mission.

———— ∞ ————

Q. When did the Oregon and California Railroad reach Ashland?

A. 1887.

———— ∞ ————

Q. Where did *Kalmiopsis leachiana,* which looks something like a rhododendron and is one of the world's rarest shrubs, first come to the attention of botanists?

A. Kalmiopsis Wilderness, in 1930.

Q. How many Oregon colleges have research nuclear reactors?

A. Two: Oregon State University and Reed College.

Q. Where was the largest gold dredge in the world located?

A. Sumpter mining district in Baker County.

Q. Rising 105 feet, the world's tallest black cottonwood can be found where?

A. Willamette Mission State Park.

Q. What is Oregon's state bird?

A. Western meadowlark.

Q. From 1935 to 1954, how much gravel did the Sumpter gold dredge move in an average month?

A. 280,000 cubic feet.

Q. When was the Astoria-Megler Bridge dedicated, replacing the ferry for motorists crossing the Columbia River?

A. August 27, 1966.

Q. Why was the Columbia River Highway considered a significant engineering feat in 1922?

A. It was an early application of cliff-face road building applied to automobile highway construction.

Q. What warming hut is situated on Mount Hood about 1,000 feet higher than Timberline Lodge?

A. Silcox.

———∞———

Q. What was the coldest temperature ever recorded in Oregon?

A. Minus-54 degrees Fahrenheit, February 10, 1933, in Seneca.

———∞———

Q. How long did it take to build Bonneville Dam?

A. Four years (1933–1937).

———∞———

Q. How were the soles of the first Nike track shoes made?

A. Coach Bill Bowerman poured rubber over a waffle iron to produce new shock-absorbing running shoes for the University of Oregon track team.

———∞———

Q. What is Oregon's state tree?

A. Douglas fir.

———∞———

Q. Hikers in the Cascades risk exposure to what malady?

A. Lyme disease, which is carried by ticks.

———∞———

Q. What main species of tree is found east of the Cascades?

A. Ponderosa pine.

Q. How many species of plants can be found in the 80,000-acre Kalmiopsis Wilderness?

A. Approximately 1,400.

———∞∞∞———

Q. When was the toll removed on the Astoria-Megler Bridge?

A. Christmas Eve 1993.

———∞∞∞———

Q. Who is the only person to receive two unshared Nobel prizes?

A. Linus Pauling, a Nobel Laureate in 1954 (chemistry) and 1964 (peace).

———∞∞∞———

Q. How many car ferry crossings remain on the Willamette River?

A. Three (Canby, Wheatland, and Buena Vista).

———∞∞∞———

Q. What portion of Oregon's forests are publicly owned?

A. Sixty percent.

———∞∞∞———

Q. Why was production of the Tektronix 511 oscilloscope significant?

A. It was an important tool in the early development of television and computers.

———∞∞∞———

Q. What was the deepest accumulation of snow recorded in the state?

A. 246 inches, March 19, 1950, at Timberline Lodge.

Q. What was the former name of Oregon Health Sciences University?

A. University of Oregon School of Medicine.

———∞∞∞———

Q. For what contribution did Linus Pauling win the Nobel Peace Prize?

A. Trying to effect a ban on nuclear testing.

———∞∞∞———

Q. Where is the World Forestry Center located?

A. Washington Park in Portland.

———∞∞∞———

Q. What exhibit greets visitors entering the World Forestry Center?

A. A 70-foot "talking tree."

———∞∞∞———

Q. Discovered in 1902, the Willamette Meteorite weighed how much?

A. 13.5 tons (largest meteorite ever found in the United States).

———∞∞∞———

Q. What do many believe would be the most likely cause of an earthquake in Oregon?

A. Shifting of the Juan de Fuca tectonic plate.

———∞∞∞———

Q. What popular crustacean is caught in shallow water and canned in Oregon?

A. Dungeness crab.

Q. According to myths of northwestern Native Americans, what animal helped God in the creation of the world?

A. Beaver.

Q. Where can one find the only mainland breeding site for Stellar sea lions?

A. Sea Lion Caves at Hecata Head.

Q. How many waterfalls in excess of 100 feet are in Silver Creek State Park near Silverton?

A. Five.

Q. What medicinal compound is found in castoreum, the secretion given off by beavers to mark territory?

A. Salicylic acid (the main ingredient of aspirin).

Q. Where can Columbian white-tailed deer be found?

A. On a three-island preserve in the lower Columbia near Westport and Roseburg (fewer than 1,000 exist).

Q. The world's tallest Sitka spruce, at 206 feet, can be found where?

A. Seaside.

Q. What is Oregon's state rock?

A. Thunder egg, an agate (Oregon's high desert and the Ochoco Mountains contain most of the nation's supply).

Q. What is the inventory of fishbearing waters in Oregon's national forests?

A. More than 20,000 miles of streams and 170,000 acres of lakes and reservoirs.

Q. How many chairlifts serve the Timberline ski area?

A. Six.

Q. What is the state flower?

A. Oregon grape.

Q. What town boasts the nation's only municipal elevator, by which residents who are walking to work can commute "down the bluff"?

A. Oregon City.

Q. Why is the mountain beaver misnamed?

A. The animal doesn't live in the mountains.

Q. In 1848 how long did it take to travel the 16 miles from Hillsboro to Portland?

A. Two days, if the ground was muddy.

Q. When did the Portland Plank Road open?

A. March 1851 (the route is now called Canyon Road).

———∞∞∞———

Q. Where is the state's major nesting area for osprey?

A. Crane Prairie Reservoir, southeast of Bend.

———∞∞∞———

Q. What natural feature was inundated when the Bonneville Dam raised the water level in the Columbia River?

A. Cascade Rapids, an important salmon-fishing spot.

———∞∞∞———

Q. How fast can razor clams found along Oregon's coastal beaches burrow through wet sand?

A. One inch per second.

———∞∞∞———

Q. What is another name for the osprey?

A. Fish hawk (due to its feeding habits).

———∞∞∞———

Q. Where is the University of Oregon's Pine Mountain Astronomical Observatory?

A. Forty miles east of Bend, off U.S. 20.

———∞∞∞———

Q. What is the chief predator of sand dollars found in coastal waters?

A. Starfish.

Q. What were the original names of the Three Sisters mountain peaks?

A. Faith, Hope, and Charity.

———∞———

Q. Why do slugs thrive in western Oregon?

A. High rainfall and low-calcium soil.

———∞———

Q. What is a popular place for eagles to winter?

A. Klamath Basin Wildlife Refuge.

———∞———

Q. According to legend, Face Rock, a sea stack on the south coast near Bandon, is actually what?

A. The face of an Indian maiden enchanted by an evil sea spirit.

———∞———

Q. What is the osprey's only natural enemy?

A. Eagles.

———∞———

Q. What gelatinous algae, a delicacy in China and Japan, grows in an isolated pond north of Medford?

A. Mare's eggs.

———∞———

Q. Where are the Koosah and Sohalle Falls?

A. McKenzie River.

Q. How many Oregon rivers are designated Wild and Scenic?

A. Forty-five, including several branches of the same river.

————— ❧ —————

Q. In the late 1980s, before it became a National Monument, how much geothermal power did the Bonneville Power Administration estimate could be generated from Newberry Crater?

A. 1,500 to 2,000 megawatts per hour (more energy than is produced by Bonneville Dam).

————— ❧ —————

Q. Sometimes called a sea parrot, what bird that summers in Oregon can be identified by its thickset black body, white breast, and red legs and bill?

A. Puffin.

————— ❧ —————

Q. What happened to Mount Mazama?

A. After the volcanic peak's eruption, its caldera filled with water, becoming what is known as Crater Lake.

————— ❧ —————

Q. What is the life span of the banana slug, a much-too-frequent visitor to Oregon gardens?

A. Six years, during which it may grow up to 10 inches long.

————— ❧ —————

Q. What is a "Cooper vane"?

A. A device on Boeing 727s that prevents the rear exit from being opened in flight (named for skyjacker D. B. Cooper, who in November 1971 boarded a flight in Portland and exited the aircraft at 10,000 feet with $200,000 and a parachute, never to be seen again).

Q. The bull Stellar sea lions that inhabit the Sea Lion Caves near Florence can weigh how much when fully grown?

A. Up to one ton.

Q. What, according to many scholars, was most responsible for advancing the science of bridge-building?

A. Railroads, which required structures capable of supporting heavy loads moving at a rapid pace.

Q. Most aquatic birds dive only a foot or two below the surface to obtain food, but how deep can Oregon's water ouzel (dipper) dive?

A. Approximately 15 to 20 feet.

Q. What is the only venomous reptile that inhabits Oregon?

A. Western rattlesnake.

Q. The rare *Iris innominata,* which can be found in the Kalmiopsis Wilderness in Josephine County, blooms in what colors?

A. Bronze, yellow, and purple, with veins a deeper shade of the petal color.

Q. What amphibian less than two inches long can be heard on warm spring nights from the timberline to the dune grass of the coast?

A. Green tree frog, sometimes called the "chorus frog."

Q. Of his many contributions, which did the public most associate with Linus Pauling?

A. Megadoses of vitamin C for improved health and as a cancer preventative.

———∞———

Q. What landmark can be found 20 miles east of Springfield in Lane County?

A. Gibraltar Mountain.

———∞———

Q. Where may one take classes in desert ecosystems, bird watching, and Native American stone tools?

A. Malheur Field Station near Princeton.

———∞———

Q. What is the primary source of food for the sage grouse?

A. Sagebrush, which also provides the bird with nesting material and shelter from predators and weather.

———∞———

Q. On October 12, 1962, what came ashore at Crescent City and blew down the Willamette Valley to strike Portland during the daily rush hour?

A. Columbus Day Storm.

———∞———

Q. How many cougars remain in Oregon?

A. About 2,000.

Q. What large and often destructive ocean wave is generated by an earthquake?

A. Tsunami.

Q. What primary factors did Intel consider in 1974 when the company built a facility in eastern Washington County?

A. Reliable sources of waterpower, quality universities, low housing costs, and the cultural amenities of Portland.

Q. The Pacific Coast Trail was established in 1928, but in what year did hikers first travel the entire distance from Mexico to Canada?

A. 1972.

Q. A traveling exhibit hall, five permanent halls, a five-story-tall Omnimax Theater, the Murdock Sky Theater, and a diesel submarine are all components of what educational facility?

A. Oregon Museum of Science and Industry in Portland.

Q. How far inland does the Juan de Fuca plate extend?

A. Cascade Mountains.

Q. When constructing the historic Columbia River Highway, how did engineers place a roadbed on the steep, unstable hillsides near Multnomah Falls?

A. Sidehill viaducts anchored one side of the roadbed to the hill; the other side was supported by columns.

Q. What defense does *arion aterrufus,* a type of slug often found in Oregon, employ against birds?

A. Once caught, it curls into a ball in the bird's throat, forcing the bird to spit it out or choke.

———✠———

Q. Where can puffins be seen in the state?

A. In large colonies on coastal rocks near Tillamook, Bandon, and elsewhere along the coast during the summer.

———✠———

Q. Prior to its last eruption in the early 1800s, how much taller was Mt. Hood than it is today?

A. An estimated 500 to 1,000 feet.

———✠———

Q. What Oregon wildflower has three long, symmetrical white petals set in the middle of three leaves?

A. Trillium.

———✠———

Q. Two tall rocks in Douglas County south of Crater Lake were the inspiration for naming what body of water?

A. Rabbitear Creek.